A Survival Guide for Child Care Providers:

Tips from the Trenches

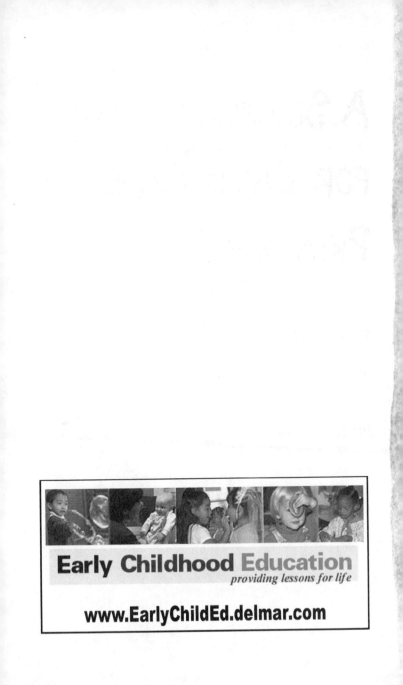

Early Childhood Education
providing lessons for life

www.EarlyChildEd.delmar.com

DELMAR

THOMSON LEARNING

A Survival Guide for Child Care Providers
by Karen Levine

Business Unit Director: Susan L. Simpfenderfer	**Executive Production Manager:** Wendy A. Troeger	**Executive Marketing Manager:** Donna J. Lewis
Acquisitions Editor: Erin O'Connor Traylor	**Production Editor:** J.P. Henkel	**Channel Manager:** Nigar Hale
Editorial Assistant: Alexis Ferraro		**Cover Designer:** DC Designs

For permission to use material from this text or product, contact us by
Tel   (800) 730-2214
Fax   (800) 730-2215
www.thomsonrights.com

Library of Congress Cataloging-in-Publication Data

Levine, Karen
 A survival guide for child care providers: tips from the trenches / by Karen Levine
   p. cm.
 Includes index.
 ISBN D-7668-5001-3
1. Child care--Handbooks, manuals, etc. 2. Child care workers--Handbooks, manuals, etc. I. Title
HQ77B.5.148 2001
 362.7–dc21   2001047560

NOTICE TO THE READER

A SURVIVAL GUIDE
FOR CHILD CARE
PROVIDERS

TIPS FROM THE TRENCHES

by Karen Levine

DELMAR

™

THOMSON LEARNING

Australia   Canada   Mexico   Singapore
Spain   United Kingdom   United States

Dedication

*I dedicate this book to Jan Miller
and Peggy Sradnick:*

*Jan for the extraordinary vision
that led her to create Basic Trust;*

*and Peggy for the sensitivity
to pick up the ball and keep it
rolling with her own special spin.*

Acknowledgments

I am enormously grateful to all of the child care providers who shared their experiences with me. I am particularly grateful to Mary DeBey and Wendy Rolnick, good and generous friends who have spent their professional lives pursuing all that is best for children, and who are eager to share their knowledge with anyone who has the interest of children at heart. And, as always, I am thankful for the help of my lifelong friend and partner, Alan Gelb, without whom I would not have been able to write this book or raise our two remarkable sons.

The author and Delmar would like to express their gratitude to the following professionals who offered numerous, valuable suggestions:

Jody Martin
Children's World Learning Centers
Golden, Colorado

Irene Cook
Taft College's Children Center
Taft, California

Fran Young
Great Beginnings Child Development Center
Pennsauken, New Jersey

Contents

Chapter 1

DISCOVERING CHILD CARE

Twenty-one years ago, when my oldest son Noah was six months old, my husband and I were feeling desperate. We lived in a small apartment in New York City and both worked at home. We'd been through a few baby-sitters but we didn't love any of them, and our home was too small to accommodate three adults and a very loud, active baby. Then a friend mentioned a child care center called Basic Trust that was just a few blocks south of us. She said it had been started by a woman named Jan Miller who was absolutely brilliant when it came to kids.

I must admit that I had my doubts when I took Noah to visit Basic Trust for the first time. I was worried about how my precious baby boy would have his needs met by caregivers who had to take the needs of lots of other babies into account. But when I met Jan, my concerns disappeared. First of all, she was surrounded by an incredibly happy looking group of children. Everyone at Basic Trust was busy, teachers as well as kids. Everyone was talking and working and creating and connecting. Noah was absolutely enthralled by the scene.

Jan welcomed us both and began telling us about her philosophy of child care. At its heart was the belief that babies were meant to be with other babies. Just as important was her conviction that caregivers—parents, grandparents, and baby-sitters— thrived when they were part of a community. "We all nurture each other," she said quite matter-of-factly, "and the babies are the big winners."

That was the beginning of my experience with child care. Noah was at Basic Trust until the end of his third year when he and all of his buddies moved on to pre-Kindergarten in the elementary schools they would attend for years to come. While at Basic Trust, we had monthly parent meetings where we discussed whatever we were going through with our children: everything from sleep deprivation to how to handle a tantrum. All of the parents spent an enormous amount of time with each other, meeting in play-grounds over weekends and entertaining each other's children. During those three years, the caregivers, kids, and other parents at Basic Trust became our extended family.

My involvement with Basic Trust, however, went well beyond my experience as a parent at the center.

I became fascinated by the whole process of child development, and Jan nurtured my interest while she nurtured my son. I had worked for years as a journalist, and soon after Noah began child care, I wrote an article for *Parents Magazine* about Basic Trust and our choice to put him in group care. That article led to another, and before I knew it, my magazine writing became focused on child development, parenting, and child care issues. In time, I became a Contributing Editor at *Parents Magazine* and launched a column called "The Working Life" that dealt with the issues of dual-career families.

When Noah was six, Nathaniel was born, and we headed straight to Basic Trust where Nat had a blissful first year. But then we had to move. We left the city when Nat was 18-months old and moved to a small town in upstate New York. My biggest concern about the move was how I would ever find another place like Basic Trust.

In fact, I never did. I found something entirely different but every bit as wonderful in its own way. I had learned by then, that what I wanted for my baby was a loving, secure environment that would nurture his imagination, and offer him lots of opportunity to play and be with other children. I wasn't interested in placing my 18-month old in a child care center that drilled him on ABCs. I wanted a place where someone would hold him on his lap and read books to him.

After some searching, I found a wonderful woman named Naureen Perkins who provided family child care in her home. Naureen was the mother of four; her youngest was Nathaniel's age and her eldest was two years older than Noah. She never had the kind of group parent meetings that Jan had, but because we lived in a small town and because our kids adored each other's company, we soon bonded with many of the families who brought their children to Naureen's.

Naureen had a big barn with chickens, goats, rabbits, and peacocks, and Nat and his friends created a world out there for themselves. All winter long, she'd bundle them up and get them outside. Other than an occasional special movie on a rainy day, the television was never on. The children cooked with Naureen and did art projects. At some point, they spent months rehearsing a big circus that they performed for the parents. Nat wore water wings under a big T-shirt and was the "strongest man in the world." We still cherish the video.

Both of my boys are still close friends with many of the children from their early child care years. I learned from Jan and Naureen, and all of the other child care providers who worked with my children, that there are many, many different ways to create a loving, nurturing child care environment. The key factor is a provider who is passionate about the work and passionate about children.

Sometimes, it can be a struggle for a child care provider to hold on to those passions. For starters, tending to the needs to children can be exhausting. Couple that with the fact that the day-in, day-out work of caring for children is not highly valued in our culture: child care providers earn low salaries and very few benefits, and it's no wonder that the burnout rate is high.

What can early child care providers do to retain the joy of their work and fight burnout? For starters, they can learn from each other. No one is better equipped to offer support and advice to child care providers than other child care providers who are down in the trenches, wiping noses, and dealing with the emotional ups and downs of young children and their parents.

This book is a compilation of hints, tips, and advice from child care providers all over the country. As a writer, I gathered this information and then organized it in a way I thought would be useful, but I never tampered with the information given to me by experts like yourself. I am not an expert. I am a grateful parent who has benefited enormously from the kind of thinking that fills the pages of this book.

All of this nitty-gritty advice, however, needs to be placed in the context of broader, more sweeping principles. In 1996 when I wrote *Keeping Life Simple,* I developed seven principles to help people determine what they most valued in their lives and to figure out a way to make room for those things. The very same principles can be applied specifically to early childhood providers who want to hang on to the passion that led them to work with children in the first place.

Seven Guiding Principles

Once you've read through these principles, it's important to do what you can to keep them in mind. You can post them on your wall or write them on index cards and stuff them in your pocket. Or you can turn them into a song and sing them to yourself. The goal here is to develop a healthy perspective, to have fun, and to remember, at the end of a day, what it is you love about your work.

Principle #1   Relax Your Standards

For people who deal with young children, there are certain standards that should never be relaxed. Safety, for example, can never be compromised. Sensitivity to children's needs can never be compromised. But there are times when too much emphasis on standards gets in the way of the bigger, more important, picture. Anyone who works with young children needs to maintain enough flexibility to see each child on his own terms and accommodate individual differences.

Consider the caregiver who wants all of her three-year olds to put on their own boots, coats, hats, and mittens when they go outside to play in the winter. Her feeling is that as long as children are physically capable of doing things for themselves, they should do it. Most certainly, the payoff in self-esteem for three-year olds who can take care of themselves in this way is a big one. But what about the three-year old who is perfectly capable of dressing himself, but who needs the reassurance of one-on-one with his caregiver before he heads out into the snow? Maybe the way he gets that reassurance is by having his caregiver zip him up or snap on his boots.

Consider a two-year old who has very specific and selective tastes when it comes to food. Her caregiver prides herself on the well-rounded nutritional meals she provides, and mealtime has turned into something of a battleground. Unfortunately, by focusing on her high nutritional standards, she's missing an opportunity for lots of wonderful interactions with this child, interactions that just might have the side effect of sparking her interest in food. When children and caregivers sit together to share a meal, children learn all kinds of social skills. They engage in conversation. They learn about table manners and they learn about the fact that people are different, with different tastes and preferences.

A caregiver who is willing to think about young children in terms of their individual growth rather than measure them exclusively against a standard is less likely to burn out.

Principal #2 Free Yourself of Stereotypical Thinking

People who care for young children always need to be aware of stereotypes. This is as true when it comes to communicating with parents and fellow workers as it is when it comes to your involvement with children.

The children you care for are actively involved in the process of discovering themselves. They do this by trying on lots of different hats to see how they feel. When child care providers create environments that are as free as possible from stereotypical casting, kids feel safe enough to try on *any* hat they want.

That kind of safe, open environment should extend to your dealings with parents as well as children. There are all kinds of subtle ways in which we classify people based on gender, race, religion, careers, and more. Parents often start out feeling uncomfortable with the people who care for their children. They worry about being judged. They worry about whether they are perceived as "good enough" parents. They worry about what you think about people "like them."

One way to safeguard against stereotyping is by addressing it regularly at staff meetings. The more comfortable staff is talking about issues like this, the easier it will be for them to alert themselves to any stereotypical thinking.

Principle #3 Take Time to Figure Out What You Find Most Satisfying

When you are dealing with young children, routine can be a good thing: it's reassuring and helps children feel comfortable and at home. The flip side of routine, however, is that you sometimes begin to feel like a robot, moving through your day without thinking much about what you're doing.

Mihaly Cziksentmihalyi, Ph.D., Professor of Psychology at the Drucker School of Management at Clermont Graduate University did a study with adolescents where he outfitted them with beepers that went off eight times a day over the course of one week each year. Each time the beeper signaled, they'd report in to him about what they were doing and how they were feeling about it. Among other things, he found that when people are involved in an activity they enjoy, they develop a sense of flow, a great feeling of energy that makes them want to continue doing what they're doing and return to it whenever possible.

In Chapter 2, we will offer a tool and a technique to help you figure out just which activities give you a sense of flow. We will help you assess how you spend your time and how you feel about what you're doing. We will take you through your day—before, after, and during work—and analyze where you feel most satisfied and where least. This kind of honest assessment is a critical step you should take before moving on to Principal #4.

Principle #4 Create Time for the Things You Care About

The idea of shifting your time and energies to accommodate the things you most enjoy seems like common sense, but you would be surprised how few people actually do it. Most of us have a "can't do" attitude when it comes to changing our patterns although it's usually something that can be done.

Suppose you discover that you feel most ready to greet kids after you've had a full half-hour of quiet time to sit, read the paper, and sip your coffee. Or suppose you discover that you're in a better mood all day long if you've been able to take a walk before your workday begins. You may learn that by shifting morning chores with your spouse and children, you can free up the time you need. Or you might decide to set your alarm a half-hour earlier every morning.

With regard to work, you may discover that you hate fixing lunch but you love music activities. If you are lucky, a coworker will have the opposite preferences and you will be able to trade off tasks. Or it might be worthwhile having the children bring in bagged lunches one day a week to take the pressure off. One worker who hated food preparation actually had the kids bring *her* a sandwich one day a week! Each person's preferences will be different. The key is to begin thinking about how you can best meet your needs because when your needs are met, you will be better equipped to meet the needs of others.

Principle # 5 Learn to Enjoy What's in Front of You

There's a Buddhist practice called "mindfulness" that teaches the value of focusing on what is beautiful in the here and now, and living in that moment. Learning to develop this kind of vision goes a long way toward clearing away the clutter in our lives. It's a valuable skill for anyone, but it's particularly important for people who work with children.

Children instinctively live in the here and now. When a three-year old says, "You never give me candy," even though you gave her a chocolate bar a few hours earlier, it's because she is completely living in the moment.

This ability children have to live in the moment can drive parents and caregivers crazy, but there is something to learn from it as well. Look around a room filled with children and focus on a wonderful interaction between two kids in the block corner. Watch a two-year old as he approaches a piece of paper with a paint brush. Listen closely as a group of three-year olds immerse themselves in a fantasy world they have created. All of it is magic, and the more pleasure you take in it, the better equipped you'll be to get through the day's rough spots.

And when you notice something particularly wonderful, tell your coworkers about it and don't forget to share it with the parents. Delight is contagious. It puts everyone in a great mood.

Principle #6 Learn to be Flexible

Peg, a child care provider from Rhode Island, remembers once gathering her group of three-year olds around her for circle time. "I had all kinds of things planned for us to talk about," Peg said. "I had clipped some magazine pictures, made a special tape, and really gave lots of thought to circle time that day."

Of course, nothing went as planned. "The children just weren't focused on me. There was lots of wiggling and giggling, and I found myself being very annoyed by it." Finally, Peg produced a picture she'd found of a mama kangaroo with a tiny, tiny baby in its pouch, and held it up for everyone to see. One of the little girls raised her hand, and when Peg asked for her comments, she stood up, looked at the group of her classmates sitting in a circle, and said, "We're making an 'O'."

Peg was blown away. "Here I was with this great picture, and she was completely on another planet. My first impulse was to pull everyone back to what I had in mind, but then I stopped and asked myself why I was working so hard to get them someplace they weren't interested in going." Instead, Peg took their lead. Circle time was a great success because she was willing to be flexible, and flexibility is an invaluable asset when it comes to kids.

In order to remain flexible, you often have to remind yourself that the goal of your time together is for everyone to have a good time, to feel safe and secure, and to look forward to what tomorrow will bring. With that in mind, it is much easier to hang on to your flexibility.

Principle #7 Prioritize

Once you know what you have to do, and what you *love* to do, it's time to prioritize and get rid of all the unnecessary, energy-sapping tasks that you dread. You'll be shocked by just how much choice you have about where to invest your efforts. Remember to keep track of what you do with your time. Ask yourself:

o   What do I need to do to take care of myself that absolutely no one else can do? For example, do I need to meditate at the end of a long day dealing with needy toddlers and parents? Do I need to make dinner plans with friends from the child care center to cement my relationship with them?

o   What can I put off for the moment and take care of later? For example, can I take care of book-mending at home when I don't feel the demands of the children? Can I sort out old toys after all the children have gone home?

o   What am I doing that someone else can do in my place? For example, can I teach someone else to make my macaroni and cheese rather than always being the chef? Why can't I allocate tedious, time-consuming tasks like billing, sorting through the lost and found, and keeping track of our shopping lists?

Perhaps the most important principle for people who work with children to keep in mind is that we all have choices, and we all can take responsibility for the choices we make. After all, isn't that what we try to teach the kids?

Chapter 2

STAYING ON TRACK

very parent knows that when you ask a child how his school day was, he'll say, "Fine." And when you ask him what he did at school, he'll say, "Nothing." It's frustrating. You want details. You want to hear about something interesting that happened. You want to know how he felt about his day, what he loved and what he hated; and what made him feel great and what disturbed him.

Although we think of the way children respond as a "kid-thing," the truth is that the days become blurred for most of us. When someone says, "How ya' doing?" we usually answer with, "Fine"—just as our children do—even if we've had a bad day. We crawl into bed with a general feeling of contentment or discontent, but we don't really think about how we spent our waking hours unless we absolutely have to.

In this book, we are proposing some serious record-keeping. Most of us spend sixteen out of every twenty-four hours awake and active. Some of the things we do make us feel great. We come away from those activities feeling energized and happy, feeling what Mihaly Cziksentmihalyi calls a sense of "flow." But we all spend time doing things we dread, or things that leave us feeling unnerved, tired, or depressed.

In many instances, we just don't have any choice about what we do. We all need to do some of the donkey work of life. But we are convinced that we actually have more control over our lives than we give ourselves credit for. The key is to begin thinking about what it is that we do with our time and how best to keep track of our feelings. Once we've done that, we can begin to think about taking charge.

This book is very focused on simplifying and improving the professional life of people who work with young children. To that end, however, it is important to think about how you spend your time before and after work, as well as at work. There's a direct emotional link from one sphere of your life to the other.

One woman named Alice, who worked in the toddler room of a child care center in Rochester, New York, told me that for years, she'd come home from work, fix dinner for her family, then sack out in front of the television. "I felt so drained at the end of the day," Alice said. "The only thing I could think about doing was vegging out." At some point, a friend of Alice's suggested they audit a class together at a local university. "It was a class about movies," Alice explained. "We'd meet twice a week, watch some classic movie, and have a really good discussion about it."

At first, Alice couldn't imagine getting out at night. But her friend pushed, and she finally caved in and went. "What happened totally surprised me," Alice said. "I just loved the class. I loved the group discussion. It was incredibly stimulating. I'd come home feeling so charged and excited. And even though I was getting less sleep than I used to, I felt much more energized."

Alice came to learn that after spending so much time with toddlers, it was important to give herself some grown-up time, time to talk and think in a completely different way, and time to nurture a different aspect of her character.

This is not to say that there is anything wrong with sitting in front of the television and vegging out. I am not passing judgments or making rules. If sitting in front of the television and vegging out leaves you feeling relaxed, then that is exactly what you should be doing. But if it leaves you feeling drained and tired, then it is time to find something else.

Keeping Track

In order to develop an awareness of how you feel about the way you are spending your time, you need to do some work. The pages that follow in this chapter are a workbook. Look at the chart on p. 24 and copy it into a notebook that you can keep with you throughout the day. Make sure you select a notebook that's small enough to stuff in a pocket for easy access all day long.

Ideally, you'll be creating a journal or log that portrays exactly what you do with your time. This technique works especially well if you do it for a complete week. Keeping track of your activities and feelings on the weekend can provide a valuable contrast.

It may be difficult for you to take the few minutes necessary to log activities. When you've got a baby screaming in one room and another in need of a nose-wipe, it's not going to be easy to put them on hold to make notes about your feelings. Just do the very best you can to make the notes while the experience is fresh. If you can glance at your watch and make a mental note of the time you begin and end an activity, you can always jot it down later.

Some people find it easier to make notes on a small tape recorder or dictation machine, the kind busy executives use to keep track of their thoughts throughout the day. Do whatever works, and do it as well as you can. The idea is not to create another burden in your life but to help you develop a powerful sense of awareness of the way you spend your time.

Let's take a look at the categories you will be keeping track of.

Start/Stop/Total

You will need to be conscious of the clock, from the moment your alarm goes off in the morning until you close your eyes at night. Think about your actions in terms of categories: getting ready for work; eating breakfast; commuting; greeting children and parents; musical games; blocks; lunch preparation, and so on. Look at your clock when you begin a new category and jot down the time. Do the same when you finish one activity before moving on to the next. Don't forget to include things like "conferencing with staff or friends" and the like. Don't worry about the "total time spent" until later. You don't need to burden yourself with adding and subtracting in the middle of a busy day.

Activity

This is where you note the category of your activity. The more specific you are, the more you'll learn from this log at the end of the week. If you're putting a group of children down for nap time, make a note of it. If one of the children is having a particularly difficult time going down, you may need to spend extra time with him one on one. Make a note of that. It may impact on how you deal with nap time from here on in.

It is also a good idea to think as specifically as possible about what you are doing. When you put the children down for naps, do you sing? Do you rub their backs? Do you put on music and listen to it yourself? Do you read them books? Remember, the goal is to learn about what you most enjoy doing, and the more details you can provide in this log, the more informative it will be when you review it at the end of a week.

Don't forget to include your nonwork activities in this log. Do you drive to work? Do you listen to the radio? Do you stop and fill up the tank on the way to work, or is that something you do later in the day? When your children get home from school, do you nag them about schoolwork? Do you play games with them?

Everything that is part of your day should find its way into this log. And remember, this is not something you're being graded on. You are the sole contributor and you are the only one who will read it. The goal is to learn about yourself, how you spend your time, and how you feel during the course of a day.

Teachers are very busy and sometimes even burdened by their responsibility. Maintaining this log should never feel like an additional burden. The goal is to make your life easier, and despite the extra effort this will require for a short time, ultimately it will go a long way toward meeting that goal. Hang in there and do the best you can with it. The best you can do will be good enough.

Feelings

It is best to jot down your feelings soon after you've finished an activity. The closer you are to the feelings, the less likely you will be to edit them, consciously or unconsciously. You don't need to write long, detailed notes here. A few words, if they're well chosen, are fine. Sometimes it helps to think in terms of "feeling" words. At other times, it helps to think in terms of opposites such as happy/sad, relaxed/tense, worried/ optimistic, loving/angry, gentle/tough, youthful/old, energetic/tired, interested/bored, worried/carefree, and agitated/calm.

It's also important in this section to think about how much of a sense of satisfaction you get from what you're doing. We all do things that aren't nec- essarily fun but that offer us a sense of satisfaction. For some, that might involve preparing lunch for a group of children. I love to cook for people I care about. It fills me with a sense of well-being. Others may derive that same sense of satisfaction from playing with children or putting them down for a nap, rubbing their backs, and singing softly. Still others may get their greatest sense of satisfaction from interacting with parents and helping them get through a difficult time with their children.

Once you figure out what it is that creates a sense of well-being for you, you'll be in a position to think about how you can adjust your schedule to make the most of that activity and make the least of the ones you find least satisfying. It might require swapping responsibilities with fellow workers, but you might be surprised to learn that they love doing exactly what you like least.

Remember not to think too much when you write down your reactions. Your gut response is probably the most reliable. Also, keep in mind that this log is for your eyes (and your use) only. You don't need to think about how others will feel about your reactions. This is a tool to make your life simpler and more enjoyable. Again, it's not something you're being graded on.

Efficiency

Anyone who works with children knows that it isn't always wise to worry about efficiency. It might take a determined three-year old four times as long to get her own shoes on than it would take you to put them on, but the time is well-spent if she is determined to get the job done on her own. One director of a child care center in New York City has become very interested in blocks recently: how the children use them, how they interact while they're building, and so on. Cleanup used to be a big chore until she began thinking of it as "unbuilding." "I was so worried about getting the job done," she said, "that I overemphasized it as a chore. But when I realized that it was all about sorting, it became very different. We set up our block shelves so that the silhouette of a block was painted on the shelf where it belonged. The kids loved unbuilding. They have races with each other to see who can get it done faster." In fact, this new perspective made it possible to get the job done much more efficiently.

But there are many tasks involved in running a child care center that benefit enormously from an effort to be more efficient. Think about the way you communicate with parents, the way clothing and toys are organized, the way food and supplies are ordered, the way schedules are arranged and communicated, and the way you deal with state agencies.

There will be many entries in your log where efficiency isn't relevant. There may be times when the most efficient way of doing something isn't nearly as satisfying as a less efficient way. For example, I much prefer to chop things with a knife on a cutting board than to put them in my food processor. It takes longer, but I love the process and the good smells, and the sound of the knife cutting through a crisp clove of garlic or stalk of celery. If efficiency doesn't apply to a given task, just write NA (not applicable) in your log. Otherwise, make an effort to rate your efficiency on a one-to-five scale.

What's My Role?

We all play many roles over the course of a day: wife/husband, mommy/daddy, chef, chauffeur, drill sergeant, disciplinarian, teacher, doctor, nurse, and the like. It is helpful to think about which roles we most enjoy and which suit us best. Make a list, somewhere in the back of your notebook, of all the roles you think you might play over the course of a week. Use it as a reference when you make your entries.

When you get up in the morning, think about the many roles you will play throughout the day. As you fill in your log, think about the role you're playing for each activity but don't write it down. This category and the next—End-of-Day Analysis—can be filled in at the end of the day when you have some quiet time to reflect.

	Activity #1	Activity #2	Activity #3
	(e.g., circle time)		
Start			
Stop			
Total			
Feelings			
Efficiency			
What's My Role?			

End-of-Day Analysis

Now for the fun! The very last thing you do each day, just before you turn out the lights, is analyze your log. This is your opportunity to learn something about yourself. And believe it or not, for many people, the results are genuinely surprising. Follow the steps below.

1 Begin by totaling up the first column, Start/Stop/Total. Add up the total for each activity and note it.

2 Review what you've written in the Activity column and read across the row to What's My Role? Think about what role you've played in each activity and note it in the appropriate place.

3 When you've filled in the entire What's My Role? column, check back to the Feelings column and think about which roles you found most pleasurable or satisfying, and which roles you found least pleasurable or satisfying. Give yourself time to think about how you might rearrange your life to maximize your time in the pleasurable roles and minimize your time in the most stressful roles. Remember, this is a time for reflection. Don't expect any miracles.

4 Look back at your Start/Stop/Total column and match it up against the Feelings column. How much time do you spend doing things that offer

you very little satisfaction? How much time do you spend doing the things you most love, the things you find most satisfying, and the things that leave you with a feeling of well-being?

5 Think about what was most surprising in your log and make a note of it. Perhaps you're surprised by how much time you spend doing things that you genuinely don't enjoy. Maybe it's the other way around. Maybe you're surprised by how much pleasure you take in being an organizer/administrator. Maybe you're surprised by how little pleasure you take in your one-on-one contact with children.

6 Repeat this process every day for a week, each day with a new log. At the end of the week, go over all of your notes, paying special attention to your End-of-the-Day Analysis. Give yourself plenty of time to think about what you're reading.

Again, the goal here is to reflect. Ultimately, you will want to find enough time in your life to do more of what you love and less of what you loathe. In order to achieve that goal, you'll need to keep track of the Seven Guiding Principles:

#1—Relax your standards.

#2—Free yourself of stereotypical thinking.

#3—Take time to figure out what you find most satisfying.

#4—Create time for the things you care about.

#5—Learn to enjoy what's in front of you.

#6—Learn to be flexible.

#7—Prioritize.

Keeping a log and being mindful of the Seven Guiding Principles is only one step toward simplifying your life as an early childhood caregiver, however. The next step involves learning lots of shortcuts and tips from your fellow caregivers. You can learn from each other how to make room for the things you most enjoy.

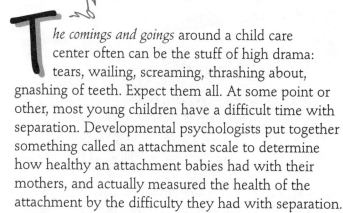

Chapter 3

PARTING IS SUCH SWEET SORROW

he comings and goings around a child care center often can be the stuff of high drama: tears, wailing, screaming, thrashing about, gnashing of teeth. Expect them all. At some point or other, most young children have a difficult time with separation. Developmental psychologists put together something called an attachment scale to determine how healthy an attachment babies had with their mothers, and actually measured the health of the attachment by the difficulty they had with separation.

The intensity with which babies say good-bye to their parents in the morning and greet them at night will vary significantly from child to child, and from month to month. There are times when separation is a developmental issue, and times when it reflects a problem at home, an ear infection, or simply a bad night's sleep. The key for child care providers is never to get caught up in the intensity of a child's separation issues. Sadness and anxiety are perfectly natural reactions to many transitions and should be treated as such.

There are, however, better and worse ways of dealing with these transitional moments, and depending on your navigational skills, you can make life easier or more difficult for children and parents. Don't forget that parents have a hard time with separation, too, especially when it involves leaving their child screaming in your arms. Let's have a look at what you can do to sweeten up the sweet sorrow of parting for everyone involved, beginning with mom and dad.

Helping Parents

Children can have a very hard time with comings and goings, but sometimes it is the parents who have an even harder time. Some parents will go through an extended "dance" of *good-bye . . . wait . . . I love you . . . wait . . . come give me a kiss . . . I love you . . . wait . . .* that makes a charged situation potentially explosive. It is important to create an understanding and a protocol with parents concerning the issue of leaving.

First off, explain to parents that a period of adjustment is absolutely normal and to be expected.

The fact that their child looks sad or nervous when they say good-bye is a healthy sign of their love. But they won't be sad and nervous all day long.

Encourage parents to use some vacation time during the first week their child is in care with you so that they can help ease their child into the new environment. They might spend a whole day with you and their child the first day, then half a day the next, and whittle their way down to an hour or so.

Always welcome parents and children, and use both of their names. "Hi Alice. Hi Max. It's great to see both of you here today." Children pick up on good vibes between you and their parents, and it makes them feel safe. Even an infant who doesn't yet have language as we know it will be able to pick up on good vibes.

Whenever possible, help parents establish a relaxed morning routine. If they can come in, give you the lowdown on anything important that's happened since they last saw you, then sit down to read a book with their child, it will make the separation easier.

Enlist parents' help by having them keep their child's home life as calm as possible during those first few weeks at the center.

Encourage parents to check in with you daily so that you can all share news about how the adjustment is going. It is important to keep the pipeline of communication open.

Explain to parents right at the beginning that there is a constructive way for them to leave their child. Parents should know that children will feel better if the parent is understanding but positive about the separation. Long, drawn-out good-byes are excruciating for babies. Parents can hang around for as long as they want, but once they make the move to go, it should be done swiftly and matter-of-factly.

It's a good idea to have a message board for parents to use. Often, in the rush of morning, you may not get to have a one on one with a parent to hear about what happened at home the night before. It could be something of significance that impacts how the separation is going to go this morning such as a restless night, a bad dream, a cold, and so on. With the parents' message board in place, parents can leave little notes about their children to keep you in the loop.

When children are having a hard time with separation, offer parents words that will be helpful: "I know it's sad for you to say good-bye to mommy, but I'm sure you're going to have lots of fun and I'll be back for you when my work is over." A statement like that acknowledges their feelings, lets them know that you're confident they're in good hands, and tells them that you'll return. All three parts of that formula are important.

Even after the initial easing-in period, it is a good idea to encourage parents to spend some time with their child at the center when dropping them off. A shared book, a look at yesterday's drawing, a peek at the progress of a marigold seedling: little moments like these count for a lot. The rule of thumb is that when parents need to rush and make a quick exit, that will be the time their child has the most difficulty with separation.

Stress to parents that they should never "sneak away," even if the child is upset by their leaving. Children whose parents sneak away often spend entire days fretting or even sitting by the door, waiting for them to reappear. Encourage parents to remind their kids they have to go to work but will be back when their workday is done. Allow the child space to get over being upset and ease into interacting with the other children.

Suggest that parents give their child something of theirs to hold. One mom left her hat with her son. Kids are very sensitive to smells and they find great comfort in breathing in the "smell" of their mommy when they miss her.

If you have a big erasable board, let the parents write a little note to their child. The child can be there when the parent writes, "I love you!" and during the day, the child can go visit the message whenever she wants to.

Suggest that parents leave a "letter" to their child with their teacher that can be read at nap time.

Let the parents post a family photo on their child's cubby so the child can see it when she's homesick.

If you notice parents are stretching their good-byes out in a way that makes it difficult for children, talk to them about it privately when they're not in a hurry and not feeling vulnerable. You need to be very sensitive. Many parents feel guilty about leaving their children in the first place. They need sensitivity and care.

Helping Children

The issues that children face concerning separation are different from the issues their parents face. Lots of different approaches work when you're trying to help a child adjust to child care. You need to find one that you're comfortable with. What follows are suggestions from child care workers like yourself.

Sometimes, when a parent leaves a child, the child goes into a kind of mourning. This mourning may last only a few minutes, but, as with all cases of mourning, there is no value in trying to "jolly" somebody out of it. Instead, allow the child space and some time to get over being upset. She may want to curl up on the sofa or to sit with a favorite caregiver. Then, when she's had her time, you can ease her into interacting with the other kids.

Children have an easier time with transitions when they know exactly what to expect. In other words, establishing a routine may prove to be the best medicine. A daily routine is a kind of wristwatch to a young child. Think about how you would feel if you were taken into a limbo where there were no clocks, and no sense of when a day would end and you could be reunited with your family. The daily routine clues the child into what "time" it is and helps him predict when mom or dad will come back.

Reinforce routine by listing what you will do as the day goes along until the child's parents arrive. Go over this list as many times as she wants or as you feel is beneficial. Throughout the day, announce "signposts" that remind the child where she is exactly in the arc of the day: lunch, nap time, music time. After a while, let the child become the "announcer." She'll enjoy the responsibility and it will effectively internalize the clock for her.

Routine is never more important than right at the start of a child's experience with child care. For at least the first three weeks, hold off on any ambitious field trips until the child is really at home in the center and feels secure.

Encourage children to bring a special blanket, pillow, or "lovey" for comforting themselves during this transition time. Provide a cozy chair in a quiet zone where the child can cuddle up with that transitional object to work through the (hopefully) transitory feelings of sadness. At first, you can join the child in this zone to offer extra comfort, but, sooner than later, you'll want to help him understand that he can go there himself when he needs to.

Some children enjoy waving good-bye to mommy or daddy from the window as they leave. Indulge this, but make sure it is not an extension of that "dance" we were talking about that only extends the difficult process of saying good-bye. Make sure mom and dad know that they're not supposed to stand out there waving forever: just a quick wave and then off.

Never underestimate the power of distraction. If a child is having a very hard time saying good-bye, she might respond to a new, fresh idea. For example, you could suggest that she make a card to take home that day. And then, in the rush of collecting art materials and setting up, her sad feelings might very well take a back burner to the excited feelings that you've stirred up in her.

For an older child who's having trouble saying good-bye, you can suggest that he dictate a note to his parents if he's missing them. A variation on this would be to set up a "message board" on a blackboard or a board for erasable markers where children can post messages for their parents. They'll need you to help with the posting.

The anxiety that children can experience when they separate from their parents can be contagious. A child who is having trouble saying good-bye to mommy and daddy may have her feelings all stirred up again when she watches her friends saying good-bye to their parents. The coming and going of mommies and daddies will remind her how much she misses her own, so, if possible, distract her as best you can while these farewells are happening.

Make sure a child's cubby is his "personal place." It is not a place that other children can rifle through. Encourage parents to leave a garment of theirs with their child and help him tuck it away into his cubby, in a "safe" place, so that he can come back to it whenever he needs it.

A real "pick-me-up" in a child's day can be a little note or card that a parent packs in the child's lunch or sticks in the child's coat pocket. Suggest to parents that they do this, not necessarily every day but now and then, as a lovely surprise. Even if the child can't read, she can be read to and that "telegram" in the middle of a long day can go a long way toward feeling less lonely.

An eight-hour day at the center can feel like an extended voyage away from home to some children. Why not approach it that way, and have parents make a photo album for their children that they can keep with them for when they need to "catch up" with family members. The album should include everyone who loves them: mommy, daddy, brother, sister, aunt, uncle, cousin, grandma, grandpa, Rover, and so on. Urge parents to involve their children in the creation of the book, especially by asking who they would like to include.

Within reason, try not to start the day officially until everyone is on board. That means if you start off your day with circle time, let's say, it's best to hold off until all the children have arrived at the center. Coming in while the activity is going on will be hard for many children, and the interruption as latecomers arrive will stir up feelings in those who have already been there a while. Hang loose as long as you can!

It is important to recognize that all the special attention you are giving to a new child who is transitioning in can be resented by the children who are the old pros. This is not unlike the sibling response that inevitably occurs when a new baby comes along. You can deal with that resentment by posting photos of the old pros when they first came to you for care. Remind them of all the special little things you did with them to ease their adjustment.

The next step in neutralizing the resentment of the "old" kids toward the "new" kids is to suggest to the old pros that they help transition in the new child. They can help you get the diapers, show the new child the cubbies where clothes are kept, explain the routines around the art supplies, and so forth. You might particularly think about the right "match" for this: the right old child to mentor the right new child.

Don't forget to praise the old pros for how professional they are. Their mastering of the routine is a great help to the life of the center. Never be stingy with your positive feedback. There should be plenty to go around.

The emotional turmoil that a new child is going through can be wearing on the other children and can fray everyone's nerves. Be sure to encourage the other children to express their feelings in a constructive way. You can help relieve some of the tension by saying things like "Joey cries so much it sometimes makes me feel sad. But when he gets to know us better, he won't feel like crying any more."

We always play a story tape at nap time. We suggest that each week, parents read their child's favorite story into a tape recorder. Then, we take turns playing different tapes on different days, and have a little "visit" from mommy and daddy's voice at nap time. The kids are very excited to tell mom and dad about it at pick-up time. "You read to us at nap time today!"

One mom had a special song she always sang to her child. By the time the child was three, she sang it to herself whenever she missed her mom.

End of Day

Sure, children miss their parents when they leave in the morning, but guess what? Sometimes they have separation problems at the end of the day when it is time to go home, as well. We've all seen the spectacle of parents coming in to pick up their child and having that child run away and even hide so as not to leave the center. This can be funny (or mildly embarrassing for the parents, even though it shouldn't be), but keep in mind that it all has to do with transitions and separation that are difficult for little ones under any circumstances.

Part of the problem at pick-up involves a renewal of the feelings the children had when they left their parents. They see them and remember how much they've missed them, and they deal with it either by ignoring them, giving them a hard time, or bursting into tears. Another part of it, however, is that they've been having a great time all day and don't want it to end.

The key to making this particular transition easier for the children is to prepare them as the day draws to a close.

Don't forget the importance of wind-down time! Different caregivers have different favorite ways to settle the children for the end of day. Some prefer story time; some like music and movement. It's a "whatever works" situation for you. Just try to establish a routine.

When the children are getting ready to leave, give them a "sneak preview" of what will be coming up tomorrow: a visit to the park; a walk to the library; a stop at the bakery to buy a fresh loaf of bread. Having something to look forward to makes it easier to leave.

Just as it is helpful to have a parent stay for a few moments at the start of the day, it is helpful for them to do the same at pick-up time. Of course, it can be late and rushed in the afternoon and evening hours, but just a few moments to look at a picture that was drawn that day or a snake that was molded out of clay can grease those "going home" wheels. And it gives parents something specific to talk to their children about as they make their exit.

The transitional object that worked at the start of the day can also do the job at the other end of the day. The teddy, doll, or piece of blanket may be just what the child needs to make that passage, at least for a while.

Don't forget that the child who's leaving may want a big good-bye hug from you. And don't be stingy with your hugs. After all, you've chosen this line of work because you like children. Sadly, these days, we must balance our impulse to be physically affectionate with current child abuse training that discourages too much touching.

Taking Care of Yourself

Burnout is a constant threat to caregivers (see Chapter 13), and the pressing neediness of a child dealing with transition issues can up the burnout factor before you're even aware of it. True, caregivers develop a certain resistance to the cries of a child, but past a certain point, biological buttons are pushed and the ongoing sobbing of a bereft child can jangle anyone's nerves. The following measures may be of help to you.

Continually remind yourself that this period of anxiety is usually over in a few weeks. This, too, shall pass.

Take your breaks as you have them and as you need them. Let somebody else take over when you find yourself at the end of your rope. Everyone will understand.

Fortify yourself for that which is difficult. That means getting a lot of rest during these weeks so that you can be as patient, understanding, and loving as possible. Eat well, and steer clear of junk food and too much sugar and caffeine.

Do not rush to conclusions about the child you're dealing with. You may discover that your most challenging case soon becomes one of the best-adjusted, happiest children in your group.

Special Considerations

There are particular times in a child's life when transitions to new settings can become more intensely difficult. For example, between the ages of five and eleven months, many babies go through a period characterized by separation anxiety. By this point in their lives, they have accrued enough "streets smarts" to know that there is such a thing as a stranger, who may be anyone other than mom, dad, brother, sister, or grandma, let's say, and having that stranger nearby makes them anxious.

Transition difficulties often go through the roof with the addition of a new sibling. Even an already transitioned child may go through major regression. If you realize that a major event is occurring or is about to occur in a child's life, you might suggest to the parents that they consider postponing a child care change until this period passes.

Any loss in a child's life can set off a whole new round of separation anxiety. Having someone they love move away, or a death in the family, or even the death of a pet (and that can include gerbils!) is likely to increase a child's neediness and complicate his transitions. Be loving and supportive, and you will all get through it.

Separation Anxiety

As a caregiver, it is important that you know and understand the difference between normal feelings of sadness that may come when a child separates from his parents and the development of a phenomenon known as *separation anxiety.*

Separation anxiety usually occurs between the ages of seven and eight months when an infant is seriously bonding with his parents. Just about anyone else is seen as the "other," bringing up fears and looks of revulsion from a child that can elicit feelings of rejection. But don't let yourself get caught up in it. It is completely normal behavior that can be dealt with in a number of ways.

Hold infants when they need to be held. Even though they may not seem to like it, they really do need it.

Be generous with your attention to each individual. Don't be stingy. A lot of attention is not going to "spoil" an infant. Instead, it is going to make him feel more secure and happier, and less demanding as time goes on. Make a point of interacting individually with each infant several times a day, if only for a few minutes at a time. This is how the children in your care will come to feel special and taken care of.

Study the interaction of parents with their child and see what you can "borrow" from them. If there are elements in their interaction that troubles you, subtly try to model for them by gently explaining your actions and approaches as you go along.

See how much fun you can have with the children in your care. Fun in all its forms, particularly laughter, is probably the best way in the world to promote positive feelings.

It is helpful to offer children a change in scenery when they are having a hard time. Go for a walk, visit another classroom, or visit a new playground. All of these adventures offer a kind of distraction that is most welcomed by lonely children.

Make sure the parents understand this particular developmental stage, and recognize that it is healthy and normal, even though it can be very trying. Some parents cannot even go to the bathroom alone when their child is going through normal separation anxiety.

After you've done everything you can think of (and everything *we* can think of) to help a child, you just may have to accept defeat. There are times you'll have to settle for, "I see how sad you are that mommy had to go," and let a child be sad. It's not really a matter of crying "uncle;" it's a matter of accepting the fact that everyone—even babies—have to learn to live with all kinds of feelings. And there's nothing wrong with that.

Chapter 4

Food, Sleep, and Safety— The Basics

ood, sleep, and safety are the most basic building blocks for a nurturing environment. Let's have a look at each of them, beginning with food.

How much comfort do you get out of mashed potatoes with gravy? Macaroni and cheese? Warm apple fritters?

The answer is, a lot.

Food and comfort go hand and hand, and that goes doubly for children. But, as we all know, many negative messages get sent around food that can later become serious problems. This is an opportunity to learn something from each other about how we can deal with food as a wonderful ingredient in a child's life, a way for them to receive comfort, nutrition, and pleasure all at once.

Food for Infants

Food is a whole new world for infants: exciting, frightening, confusing, delicious. Infants need to be led gently into the world of food, and, as a caregiver, you will be one of their primary guides. There are a number of specific concerns that you'll need to keep in mind when feeding the infant in your care, whether you are using expressed breast milk or commercial formula. A lack of attention to these concerns can have serious and even dangerous results.

I know that it probably seems obvious to say this, but I think it needs to be stressed: *infants need to be supervised when they eat.* First of all, they don't have the ability to get the food they need into their systems. Secondly, they have to be carefully watched to make sure they don't choke on anything. There is no margin for error when it comes to infants and food. It only takes one second for something to get lodged in their windpipe.

I never worry about how much "real" food infants eat as long as they're getting their formula or breast milk. From a nutritional standpoint, that's really all they need between birth and six months. I try to tell this to parents all the time. Most doctors will tell you that vitamin and mineral supplements rarely are necessary unless specifically recommended by a physician.

I am completely crazy when it comes to labeling foods. You have to be. I use lots of adhesive tape marked with the baby's name. Certain children have certain nutritional needs, not to mention food allergies, and none of us can afford a mix-up in that department.

Always make sure that when a mom or dad brings in a bottle of breast milk, it is clearly labeled with the child's name on it. Remind them that "Josh," is not enough. He may be the only "Josh" in their lives, but chances are, I've got a few of them in mine!

Breast milk should be kept in the freezer until it is time for the child to be fed. Then it's best to thaw it out under cool, running water. Never warm bottles of breast milk on the stove. The milk will curdle.

Never microwave breast milk or formula. It is difficult to control and test temperatures with microwave heating. Babies have very tender mouths and throats. Milk and other liquids that have been warmed in a microwave can cause serious burns.

Always refrigerate bottles with formula until it is time for feeding. Bacteria multiplies quickly at room temperature, and babies are very susceptible to germs.

Never feed a baby any formula that has been left out of the refrigerator or that smells sour.

Wash out bottles and throw out any leftover formula after feeding. The baby's saliva can be drawn back into the bottle and stimulate the growth of bacteria. It may feel like you're being wasteful but it's really the responsible thing to do.

Sometimes, when it gets hectic, you forget to put things back in the fridge. When it comes to formula, though, you've got to keep it stored and covered in the refrigerator at all times.

I once had someone working for me who decided to stretch the formula a bit. She thought she was doing me a favor by adding a little more water than the package called for. I had to set her straight. If you don't follow the instructions carefully, the babies don't get the right number of calories and nutrients. It can be very dangerous.

If I had three tips to offer people who work with kids, they would be, "Wash your hands," "Wash your hands," and "Wash your hands." That's especially true when you are preparing to feed an infant.

Never touch the nipples with your fingers. It's a sure way to spread germs.

Never take short cuts when it comes to cleaning reusable bottles and nipples. Do it thoroughly after each use. You can stick them in the dishwasher, or, if you're washing them by hand, make sure to use very hot water and boil them for five minutes before refilling them. Better yet, use disposable bottles.

I always hold young babies when I'm feeding them. Even if you find a way to prop a bottle up so they can drink from it (and even if they can hold it themselves), it is important for them to associate their feeding with personal, human contact. Lots of eye contact and reassuring is important when you feed a baby.

Preparing Infant Foods

Always begin by washing your hands carefully with soap and water. (I'm going to say that a lot in this book, but the more caregivers I spoke to, the more I heard it.)

If you feed an infant from a jar of food, each time you put the spoon from the baby's mouth back into the jar, you're introducing bacteria from the baby's saliva into the jar. If the jar is only half finished, the bacteria breeds, even in the fridge. You can avoid the problem by pouring out a small portion of food from the jar into a small bowl, and feeding the baby from the bowl. That way, the spoon from the baby's mouth never goes into the jar, and the leftover food can be stored for future use.

It's really important to remember that any contact with your skin can contaminate an infant's food. I have the following list posted on the wall in our kitchen at the center:

o Do not touch the nipple of a bottle or the rim of a cup.

o Do not test the temperature of strained food by putting a spoon on your arm and then into the baby's mouth.

o Keep your fingers out of the jar of baby food and never taste the food with the tip of your tongue.

o If you want to test the temperature, do so by placing the container or a sample poured from it onto your wrist or inner elbow.

When it comes to baby food, go colder rather than hotter. Babies don't mind cold or room temperature foods, but they can be badly scalded by food that is too hot.

Never microwave any baby's food, liquid or solid. Microwaves leave things very unevenly heated with hot spots and cold spots. One spoonful might be cold and the next one searing hot. If you do use a microwave, make sure to stir the food so that the temperature is even throughout.

Breastfeeding: Ways to Help and Support

It is not uncommon for mothers to continue to breastfeed their children even when they go to child care. Some moms adjust their work schedules so that they can come in and nurse the baby at the child care center. Other moms may collect and store breast milk for the caregivers to use, or they may wish the care-giver to use formula during the day while the nursing continues at home in the morning and/or evening. Any combination of the above also can work. For those who are taking care of nursing babies, the fol-lowing tips may prove helpful.

Don't forget that if a baby is drinking breast milk, he'll need to be fed more frequently. Usually, he is hungry again within two or three hours.

I always try to honor a nursing mother's style. Some moms are very comfortable sitting on a couch in the main room nursing and talking while they're doing it. Others see it as a very private, intimate time between themselves and their babies. I have a nice rocker in my nap room and I always offer it to nursing moms who want privacy.

If a baby is very attached to the breast, she might have a hard time taking a bottle. It's a whole different experience and I think the sucking is very different. It sometimes helps to use a breast-shaped nipple. But sometimes I offer these babies a covered cup with a sipping spout and we skip the bottle entirely.

You need to remember that breast milk is not homogenized, and the cream separates out and rises to the top. Whenever I use breast milk that has been refrigerated, or frozen and thawed, I need to shake it well. It's usually very thin looking and sometimes even kind of blue in color, but it's rich and nutritious.

Breast milk will last up to 48 hours in the refrigerator and up to one month in the back of a freezer that stays at zero degrees.

The first time I changed a nursing baby's diaper, I freaked out. Now I know that their stool is loose, sort of like cottage cheese, and mustard-colored. It also never smells too bad.

Remember that nursing babies poop a lot! Sometimes I feel like the food goes right through them.

First-time moms are often very insecure about nursing. They can't see how much food their baby is getting and they worry. I always try to be very supportive and encouraging. It means a lot when you say, "He's really thriving on your breast milk. He's so active and alert." It reassures them.

Whenever I hear about a mom having a hard time nursing, I ask an experienced nursing mom with a child at our center to give her a call. LaLeche is great, but talking to another mom from your child care center creates a feeling of community.

Bottle Tooth Decay

Bad habits around bottle feeding have been implicated in children's tooth decay. Here are some preventive measures to keep in mind.

I've got a rule at my center: babies only can be bottle fed when they're being held. We never put children into their cribs with bottles. We hold them, if they need the bottle, then put them down without it.

We let babies fall asleep with bottles, but only if they're filled with water. Even then, we always watch carefully to take it away as soon as they drift off. If babies go to sleep with a milk bottle, the milk stays in their mouths while they're sleeping. The sugar in the milk can cause cavities in teeth just as they're forming, and that means that they'll be very fragile, in addition to being painful. Some babies have a hard time chewing because of this, and before you know it, you've got a problem eater. I always tell parents about these problems, too.

Lots of toddlers have a real attachment to their bottles, and they're subject to the same issues of tooth decay as babies. At home, they walk around with a bottle whenever they want one, but they have no trouble learning that they don't do that at their child care center. Kids are very adaptable. They learn that different places have different rules. The connection between bottles and tooth decay is as serious for toddlers and preschoolers as it is for babies.

We never let kids walk around with bottles because they end up passing their bottles around to each other and spreading all kinds of colds and infections. There's also a problem with children who are very active falling when they have bottles in their mouths.

Teething

Teething, which can occur anytime from around four months on, can have significant impact on the eating process. Teething infants sometimes will find some relief with chewable toys, including ones made specifically for this purpose. When looking for those hard foods that offer teething relief, steer clear of brittle crackers, raw vegetables, and any other substance that you think a child might choke on. Instead, use special teething biscuits, teething rings, and the kind of jelled rings that you pop in the freezer. Make sure that they're labeled.

 This may sound strange, but I find that sympathy is very helpful when I talk to a teething baby. It must really hurt to have those little teeth cutting through the gums. I talk to them about how much it hurts and how it will stop hurting soon.

 We've noticed that babies sometimes get really bad diaper rashes when they're teething. We're very attentive at diaper changes for teething babies. The last thing they need is more pain at both ends!

We always try to offer parents lots of support when their baby is teething. It's a time when no one gets much sleep. At least when they're in child care, there's lots to distract them and we can pass them from one caregiver to another. But for parents, teething often means sleepless nights with no relief.

It is important to be on your watch when you've got teething babies around because if you're not, you may end up with kids teething on each other!

Teethers will put anything into their mouths. You have to be very alert to make sure that everything they get their hands on is clean, smooth, and safe.

Teethers are big droolers which means their T-shirts always look like they're soaking wet. Soft terry bibs are a great way to keep teething babies dry. Just make sure you've got a lot of them on hand.

Beginning Solid Foods

Although breast milk and infant formula continue to be an important part of a baby's diet for the first three or four months, solid foods provide extra calories and nutrients for the older baby, and usually are introduced at around four to six months. Before this age, babies have a hard time keeping food in their mouths. They tend to push it out with their tongues, even when they don't want to. But by six months, most babies have strong enough neck muscles to control their head, and can manipulate food comfortably once they get it in their mouths. At this point, babies also are learning to sit up without the use of their hands. This means their hands are free to hold onto a spoon or pick up finger food. Even if parents are eager to push solids, it's best to wait for all of these skills to develop before beginning an adventure with food. When the time comes, here are some tips you can follow that will make the introduction of solid foods easier.

It is really important to coordinate with home when it comes to introducing solids. Keep communication open with parents. What has the baby eaten? Have there been any bad reactions? Let the parents take the lead and follow.

When I introduce solid foods, I usually work out a plan with parents. We introduce only one new food at a time. Then we wait another four or five days before trying out the next new food. This kind of slow, measured timetable allows babies to become accustomed to new flavors, and even more important, makes it possible for you to keep track of food problems that may occur such as food allergies or intolerances.

Never worry about how much food is actually getting consumed in the beginning. The key is to make eating a delightful adventure, with lots of good conversation and lots of opportunity to taste and touch.

Many people find that rice cereal is an ideal first food. It's the least likely of any grain to cause an allergic reaction. Rice cereal mixed with breast milk or infant formula will provide a balance of proteins, carbohydrates, and fats, and is a good source of iron.

At our center, we find it easiest to introduce solids when the baby is in our arms rather than in an infant seat. The baby is used to being held while she eats and it's very comforting. It tells her that this new experience is safe and even pleasurable.

Families are all very different when it comes to food. We usually encourage parents to introduce veggies when their baby is around seven months, although we always urge them to check with their pediatrician first. By that time, babies have got the hang of chewing. Mashed vegetables will encourage chewing, as will the rice cereal that you can now cut with less formula or breast milk.

Whenever we introduce a new food, we talk a lot about it. "Hmmm. This is sweet potato. It's so, so yummy. I can see that you really like it. So do I." It may sound corny but just think about how exciting it is to taste something wonderful for the very first time. When I talk about that, I really do feel excited!

When one or two teeth come in, it's time to give them something to chew on. We usually start with some nice lumpy food like potatoes, carrots, or bananas. Some child care centers sprinkle the food with sugar, but babies don't need salt or sugar, or anything like that. Their palates are hardly jaded yet. They're still really excited by the taste of each food.

It's really important to be relaxed around babies who are discovering food. They like to touch it and put it into their own mouths. It's more important to let them do that than it is for them to get every last drop into their mouths.

Look for foods that are soft but that can stay in one piece when a baby picks them up and brings them to his mouth. We make these Jell-O® jigglers using real fruit juice and gelatin. Kids love to touch it and watch it move, and there's never a choking danger because it dissolves in their mouths.

It's important to stay in close touch with parents concerning food allergies as children approach their first birthday. When you start giving them cheese, you find that lots of kids have a lactose intolerance. Sometimes, we pick up on it at the center before the family does; sometimes, it's the other way around. The important thing is to help each other out with lots of information.

We think of honey as the most natural sweetener on the planet, and it is. But honey has been linked to infant botulism and fatalities. This applies to honey used in cooking and baking as well. The botulism spores are not destroyed by regular cooking methods. Never give honey to an infant less than one year old.

The same rule that applies to honey also goes for corn syrup, used in lots of commercial baked goods preparations. Like honey, corn syrup can contain botulism spores that the digestive system of an infant cannot destroy. Check labels carefully, and avoid anything with honey or corn syrup until after a child's first birthday.

Many centers find that babies are ready to use a special cup in place of a bottle when they're around ten months old. By then, formula, breast milk, juices, and water can be given by cup, as long as the baby is interested. Hold the cup and make sure that the liquid doesn't flow too fast. By the time a baby turns one, she should be able to handle the cup on her own, and probably won't let you help her even if you want to.

Depending on the licensing regulations in your state, it can be great to have young teenagers helping in your child care center. It's safest, however, not to let them be in charge of feeding infants. There's just too much to be careful about such as choking, signs of discomfort, and the like.

No one should work in a child care center who isn't trained in antichoking techniques specifically designed for children and infants. It takes only a moment for something to get lodged in a baby's tiny windpipe, and it feels like an absolute miracle when you can do the maneuver and dislodge it. I know because I've done it.

Never be lax about choking dangers, both in terms of toys (see p. 119) and food. When you introduce solid foods, stay with foods that are soft or that will soften in a baby's mouth. That means NO raw carrots, NO nuts, NO popcorn, NO unpeeled fruits and vegetables, NO hard candies, NO pickles, NO hot dogs, and NO other hard foods.

Lots of centers prefer to make their own baby food with a food mill. They cook the same veggies for the babies as they do for the toddlers, and run it through the mill. If you want to do that, make sure that you cover the food immediately and place it in the refrigerator.

It's fine to freeze away tiny portions of homemade baby food in an ice cube tray and keep it covered in a freezer bag to prevent freezer burn. When you're ready to serve, just heat the cubes in a custard dish over boiling water. *Never refreeze thawed food.*

If you are participating in the Child and Adult Care Food Program (CACFP), use their infant meal pattern guidelines for information on specific foods and appropriate amounts. For further insights on nutritional issues, discuss infant feeding with your sponsor. Be sure to remember to have a medical exception on file if you are expecting reimbursement for anything other than the required foods.

Food for Toddlers

When it comes to food, toddlers are ready to make a quantum leap from the eaters they were in their infancy. Now food is an even greater adventure with a quest for new flavors, textures, and so on. Not all toddlers are lusty eaters, however. There are special tips for toddlers who are picky. Many experts urge us to have plenty of what they like available and not push them to eat things they don't like. Here are some pointers to keep in mind when feeding toddlers.

Don't be tricked by how mature some toddlers seem. All of them are vulnerable to choking and you've got to avoid any potentially dangerous food. That includes such things as:

o   fruits (cherries and olives) that have pits.

o   hard candies, nuts, and grapes that can become lodged in the windpipe.

o   peanut butter not served on bread or crackers

o   hot dogs, pickles, and other foods that are cylindrical in shape.

Think of a hot dog as a plug. It is shaped perfectly to stop up a young child's windpipe. If you serve them (which, given the fat and salt content, shouldn't be often), make sure you cut them in a way that changes their shape, preferably lengthwise, and then in small pieces.

Peanut butter can be a choking hazard, and it can set off a dangerous and even fatal food allergy.

No child care center should serve baked goods or anything else that is made with peanuts. Better safe than sorry.

Always complete a food allergy history with any entering parent. If a child has an allergy, post the child's name, allergy, and a picture in the classroom and in the kitchen. Never introduce a new food without first checking with parents.

Whenever possible, plan a week's menu in advance and send it home to parents for a review. If they see any problem (allergies, intense dislikes, and the like), they can let you know so that you can make substitutions.

If children bring their own lunches, make sure they are clearly labeled and go right into the fridge.

Never let kids walk around with food in their mouths. Toddlers are very active. They run and jump without even realizing they're doing it. We have a rule: *eating is allowed only at the table.*

Food as a Socializing Experience

Adults always associate mealtime with socializing. We go out for dinner with friends. We get together with someone we care about for a cup of tea or a glass of wine. We talk, laugh, and confide in each other. Children enjoy the same kind of pleasant, intimate environment when they're eating. And that includes infants. Think about how natural it is to talk to infants when you're feeding them. And think about how riveted they are on your face while they're eating. In some ways, all of this socializing is as nurturing as the food. The tips that follow help make the most of mealtime.

I always sit down with the children and eat while they're eating. It seems like such a natural thing to do. I talk about how delicious things are, or how spicy, or how sweet. And by the time they're toddlers, they're talking to me in the same way.

We always serve family style at our center. We have a big bowl of veggies, pasta, or whatever in the middle of the table, and I ask who wants what and spoon it onto their plates while we're all sitting together.

The National Association for the Education of Young Children (NAEYC) suggests self-serving for children two and above. It's a great way for kids to learn to help themselves, to develop a realistic appreciation for how much food they really want, and to develop a more general sense of competence.

We've done away with high chairs and replaced them with "low chairs," also called "me-do-it chairs" which can fit around a table, and are very safe and stable. They are made by Community Playthings and offer a great way for everyone to sit together.

As soon as the weather gets nice, we eat out in the backyard as often as possible. Sometimes we have a picnic on a blanket. Sometimes we sit around a table. It turns lunchtime into a little adventure.

About twice a year, I hold a parents' meeting that's just about food. It's a great time for parents to share their concern about things like overeating, undereating, picky eating, whatever. It always ends up being a fun evening, especially when we make it into a covered dish dinner. There's nothing better than talking about eating while you're eating!

Always welcome parents to join you at lunchtime. Kids love the idea of having a lunch guest. It's like a party for them.

Mealtime is a great time to introduce the idea of manners. As soon as children can talk in sentences, they can say sentences like "Please pass the ketchup."

In larger centers, eating is usually divided by age groups: toddlers eat with toddlers, preschoolers eat with preschoolers, and the babies eat with each other. Sometimes it's fun to mix things up. It feels more like a party.

Nap Time

Don't expect infants to conform to your schedule when it comes to naps. They need to sleep when they're tired, not when you want them to. Just look for their "sleepy" signals and put them in the crib.

Toddlers and preschoolers should get into a regular nap routine. If they're not tired, let them stay on their cots for quiet time. They should be able to take a book or a special toy from home with them to their cots.

If an infant cries when you put him down for a nap, pick him up. All of this business about letting them scream until they're exhausted seems like too much to ask of infants, especially when they're adjusting to a new child care center.

Use a backpack or snugli for a while with infants who have a hard time being put down. The more secure they are and the better they know you, the more willing they'll be to go down for a nap.

Establish a regular routine for nap time with toddlers. You might read a story and play a very soft, soothing CD. Just do the same thing every day and do not break routine, no matter what. You will find children begging for naps once you have them in the habit.

Be careful with nap time stories for toddlers. If it's too stimulating, their imaginations will run wild and they won't be able to sleep. Familiar stories are best like *Goodnight Moon.*

I once had a baby who would not sleep the entire first month he was with me. Finally, his mom brought in his car seat. All I had to do was put him in that car seat when I saw that he was tired and he'd nod off. I did it for a week, and then I put the car seat in the crib for a few days. After that we did away with the car seat and went right for the crib.

I use story tapes for preschoolers at nap time. They work best when the children know the story well. It's like going to sleep with an old friend.

I try to stay away from rubbing children's backs or staying with them until they fall asleep because they become reliant on having me there with them. It's important for them to learn to relax on their own.

Just before I leave the nap room, I give each child a little tuck-in and a hug. It sends them off feeling safe.

You have to make sure that the cots aren't all crowded together because the children will be too tempted to play with each other. I try to keep them all against walls or tucked into corners.

Each child has his or her own cot. They know which one is theirs. I have the parents bring in linen fresh and clean every Monday, along with a spare sheet in case of an accident. On Friday, they take their laundry home.

It's a good idea to allow each child at least three feet of space between cribs and cots. This private space allows them to sleep with fewer distractions, and it's also much healthier.

You can't control how long a child sleeps. If one wakes up before the others, she comes out to me and plays quietly on her own. Sometimes, we'll have a little snuggle and I'll read a book.

I always get feedback from parents on how the child's night went. If he had a hard time getting to sleep, it might mean that his nap is too long. If he had a sleepless night, he might need more nap time during the day to make up for it. Communication is very important.

It's a good idea to talk to parents about how they put their babies to sleep. You don't have to do the same exact thing—you can't when you've got a whole group of kids—but if a baby is having a rough time getting to sleep, it's good information to have.

Safety

There are safety tips running throughout this book, but safety is a subject that deserves special focus. States and municipalities have many rules and regulations to ensure the safety of babies and toddlers in child care settings. But our concern goes beyond those regulations. Consider some of these tips as you look around your child care center to assess its safety.

Seven Most Common Indoor Safety Hazards

1 Hot pots and pans.

2 Electrical outlets.

3 Prescription medications.

4 Poisons like bug sprays and cleansers.

5 Toilets.

6 Toys with small parts.

7 Stairs.

Things to Avoid

o   marbles

o   balloons

o   plastic bags

o   game pieces

o   jacks

o   toy chests with lids

o   dress-up jewelry

o   hot dogs

o   grapes

o   lollipops

o   peanuts

o   popcorn

o   olives

Other Safety Hazards

o Keep in mind that many common indoor plants such as philodendron, schefflera, pothos, diffenbachia, elephant ear, hyacinths, narcissus, daffodils, castor beans, rosary peas, and poinsettias are poisonous.

o Check all toys regularly to make sure there are no loose parts that could pose a choking hazard.

o Teach children not to run with anything in their mouths.

o Never prop up a baby bottle.

o Don't use styrofoam cups. Babies like to chew on them.

Chapter 5

ARTISTS AND BUILDERS

A day without art activities at a child care center just wouldn't feel right. Not only do children have a great time working with art materials but also the fruits of their labors are often remarkable to see. The creations of great artists like Calder, Miro, and Klee are often described as being "child-like" in their beauty. That's because children's art can be captivatingly colorful, and filled with images that are simple but arresting. Young children also appreciate the entire process of making art. The act of creating, for them, is as important as the final product.

Young children approach the block corner with the same kind of energy and creative enthusiasm as they approach art. In fact, their block structures are really like sculptures, and they'll often stand back and admire them in the way we admire a sculpture. Even when young children build houses and roadways, they are like architects, applying their art to a useful end.

Here are some ideas as to how to facilitate the work and growth of your young artists.

When young children are involved in art activities, they're developing their fine-motor skills. Working with crayons, paper, pencils, and play dough help toddlers hone those skills as they grasp, hold, pour, scoop, squeeze, and manipulate their materials in a variety of ways.

Always be sure that your art materials are safe to handle and won't be harmful if a toddler puts them in her mouth. Nice short, chubby crayons are best for nice short, chubby fingers!

Some people like to provide snacks and drinks that children can help themselves to while they "work," so their terrific concentration won't be interrupted. This won't work if children are working with paint or anything messy. But if they're coloring, a plate of cheese bits and crackers can be nice.

Help things along by joining in. When you participate, you're modeling the pleasure people of all ages enjoy when they create art. It's a good "prompt" for your children. They love to have you sit with them and join in. Don't think about it as "helping" as much as "sharing" a fun activity. Plus, it gives you a chance to create some art, something most of us rarely find time to do.

Children can start out at an easel when they're just under two. Use adjustable ones so they won't have a tough reach.

Thicken the paint a bit by adding more dry paint mix and apply it with small paint brushes, the kind you find in the paint section of your home improvement stores. These brushes are easier for little hands to hold and give bold, broad strokes of color with each brush stroke.

The foam paint brushes are great for kids to use. They're cheap, so you can buy a bag full of them, and they're very easy to wash.

Children usually like to stand when they make art. It's a very "active" kind of activity. They move around, bounce, and look at what other people are doing.

Easels, or even a high table, are excellent for active children who might not want to sit. Children can practice scribbling or sketching while standing up and moving around as they need to.

Children feel like genuine artists when they work at an easel, but that also can mean drips. Don't sweat the small stuff: drips can be cleaned up. If you're really worried about it, let the kids paint at the easel outside and then hose the easel down.

An alternative to an outdoor easel is to attach a large piece of paper to a fence with clothespins. Then let your kids loose with water-based, washable tempera and large brushes. (Make certain to keep any powdered tempera away from children to avoid any danger of inhaling.) If you're worried about damage to the fence, you can put a vinyl tablecloth behind the child's art paper. Some of the greatest artists choose to paint *au plein air,* meaning out of doors. So will your children on a nice day!

An old shower curtain or shower-curtain liner makes a great drop cloth. Ask parents to bring in any old ones they've got around the house. When they're done, hang the liner in the shower with the mess facing in. It will rinse off easily.

We still love the daddy's shirt smocks that we used when we were kids. Just crop the length and the sleeves with scissors, and you're ready to go.

Some teachers prefer to have children paint at a table rather than at an easel. They find that the drips make everyone's paintings look the same and interfere with the kids' intentions. A nice flat drawing table is one way to avoid drips.

A dry-erase board is excellent to have on hand, especially when displayed on an easel in the art center. The pens create exciting, color-filled canvasses that can be transformed immediately into something new with the swipe of a sponge. Kids also can make "notes" to their moms and dads whenever they're missing them.

The sidewalk is a great canvas, especially for a group art project. Those nice, fat sticks of sidewalk chalk are easy for children to handle. If the sidewalk chalk art is a summer project, you can have fun at the end of the day hosing it all down.

Toddlers love to fingerpaint. The fun becomes even more exciting when you make the "paint" out of instant pudding, cutting back the milk to only one cup. Let the kids help whip the mix with a wire whisk, then put the result into small plastic recyclable applesauce cups. Get out the paper—use actual fingerprint paper so it won't tear and get all ugly—and go! *Caution: before you begin, make sure there are no allergies or intolerances to dairy products among the children, and skip Pistachio nut pudding altogether so as not to run a risk to anyone who is nut-sensitive.* Vanilla works well (you can add food coloring to it if you wish) as does chocolate (again, if there are no allergies). And make sure those little hands are well-scrubbed at the start so the kids can have the pleasure of licking off the excess pudding!

Art gets messy. That's part of the fun. If going outdoors doesn't work, you can cover your tables with a tarp or a plastic tablecloth. Just tape the art paper down to the plastic so it won't slide around.

Lots of providers make a big deal about putting children's names on their artwork. There's a pride in ownership that's fun to see. But sometimes it's great fun to work on a big group project. Lay out a scroll of paper and let each child work on a section of it. Then hang it up and talk about how special things look when they all work together. It can have everyone's name on it or no one's.

Older children love the idea of tracing each other's bodies. Have one three-year old lie down on a big piece of paper and let her friend trace around her body. Then, the child whose body it is can draw clothing and hair, and all the other details.

Keep your eye out for youngsters who are eyeing other kids' work with envy. They get the idea, very early on, that some kids are "good" at art while others are "bad." The goal is to help them enjoy the process, not make judgments.

Use circle time before art to show children pictures of famous art works. Put posters of Picassos, Kandinskys, and lots of other abstract work up on the walls of the art corner. Kids can learn early to enjoy looking at art, and it really inspires them, even when they're very young.

Play music during art time. Ask the children to think about how the music makes them feel. If it makes them feel happy, they can paint a happy picture. If it makes them feel sad, they can paint a sad picture. It's a great way to learn about feelings as well as art.

If your center is big enough (this won't work as easily for family child care), keep an art corner available at all times so that kids don't have to wait when inspiration hits!

There's always an impulse to comment on children's artwork with something like, "That's so pretty." It's much better, though, to make comments that are more descriptive and less judgmental, even if your judgment is praise. Statements like "You sure love blue," "I can see how much you love art by your painting," or "That's a happy painting" help children think about their art as a means of self-expression rather than a way to please you.

Never make children do art when they don't want to.

Stories are a great inspiration for art, even for very little children. If you read a story, complete with pictures, you can suggest that they make a picture from the book.

Young children love to tell you the story of their artwork. And if you write down what they're saying, they're even happier. "This is my dog and this is my boat that my dog goes on."

Never "correct" a child's artwork. Sometimes we do it without even realizing by saying things like, "How about another color?"

We sometimes have special "color" days, like "red" day or "orange" day. Everyone makes paintings with one color. Sometimes we talk about it the day before and the children even dress up in that color.

Preschoolers love to tell stories and make their own books. Basically, they tell you a story and you write it down for them, and they illustrate it however they choose. Then they read their stories to everyone.

Pasting is great fun for children that have the small-motor control needed to handle a glue stick. Instead of using scissors, which is difficult for young children, offer them colored paper and let them tear it into the shapes they want.

Ask parents to bring you their old magazines. Cut out lots of photos of faces, cars, flowers, houses, babies, or anything else that catches your eye. If you keep the cut-outs organized in boxes (or even if you dump them all together in a big container), children can use them to make collages.

Sponges are sometimes more fun for young children to paint with than brushes. They can dip and dab, dip and stroke, or dip and squeeze.

A fun group project involves hanging a long, long sheet of paper on an outdoor fence and then letting preschoolers throw paint-dipped sponges at it. If the weather is nice, everyone can get hosed down when they're done.

Hand- and footprints make great take-home art. Children can press their hands or feet into a saucer of paint and then stamp them on paper. The project is even better when they include a message for mom and dad, and the date. It's a keeper!

Wash the styrofoam tray that fruits and vegetables come wrapped in *very thoroughly.* Then, let children draw on it with magic markers. When they're finished, cut it up into a puzzle. It's fun to make puzzles from your own artwork.

Develop a regular routine for cleaning up after art, and incorporate it into the project so that it doesn't feel like a chore. For example, we always have children rinse their brushes until they can make invisible paintings, paintings with water and no color.

Shaving cream is a great medium. Squirt some on a table top and let the kids mush it around.

They can make towers, or they can squiggle with their fingers to make a design.

Young children enjoy painting with water on a blackboard. Sometimes, they blow on the blackboard to make their paintings disappear.

We do as many group projects as we can. Children love working together on a big, big piece of paper and then covering a wall with it. It's also a great way to learn about cooperation. Waiting for a crayon you want can be hard, but it's a good lesson in patience.

We always view cleanup as a fun part of the activity. Sometimes, children actually fight about who gets to sponge off the table.

Never try to turn art into a "learning" experience. Children learn by doing, and the lessons come very naturally. The more you try to drive points home, the less likely they'll be to enjoy the "lesson" and the less enthusiastic they'll be about learning.

Never forget that all children are different and that they each need to make art in their own ways. Some do well with a great big piece of paper; others like to work on smaller sheets.

Some young children will enjoy having their own little notebook. When they make a drawing, put a date on it. By the end of the year, it will be a nice keepsake. But remember, for some very young children, a notebook is too confining.

Keeping Art Safe

o Avoid using any art supplies like tempera paint and clay that are dry, and that could be inhaled easily.

o Avoid using any materials that contain lead or other hazardous substances that can cause poisoning if ingested.

o Do not use rubber cement, epoxy, or instant glue. Use glue sticks, double-sided tape, paste, or school glue. These should have the AP or CP label. Use only water-based glues, glue sticks, and paste.

o Do not use permanent markers. Use only washable markers and avoid using scented markers that tempt children to put them in their mouths.

o   Avoid using empty film canisters for art projects because lids can be mouthed and have a potential hazard for choking.

o   When using small items such as beans, rice, or small styrofoam shapes for projects, always keep special watch because children may mouth their art materials and might choke on them. It is better to use these items only with older children.

Recipes for Art Supplies

These are some classic art recipes we've gathered from child care providers all over the country.

Nonhardening, No-Cook Play Dough

2 cups self-rising flour   2 T. cooking oil
2 T. alum   1 cup, plus 2 T. boiling
2 T. salt   water

Mix and knead.

Salt Paint

1/3 cup salt   1/4 tsp. food coloring

Spread in pan to dry before putting in shakers.

Cooked Play Dough

1 cup flour   1 T. vegetable oil
1/2 cup salt   2 tsp. cream of tartar
1 cup water

Heat until ingredients form ball. Add food coloring.

Potter's Clay

1/2 cup flour   1 cup salt dissolved in
1/2 cup cornstarch   3 3/4 cups of boiling water

Blend flour and cornstarch with enough water to make paste. Boil water and salt. Add to cornstarch mix and cook until clear. Cool overnight, then add 6 to 8 cups of flour and knead until you have the right consistency.

NOTE: Keep a metal salt shaker full of flour handy for the children to keep their clay from sticking.

Iridescent Soap Bubbles

1 cup of water (hard   1 T. glycerin
  or soft)   1/2 tsp. sugar
2 T. liquid detergent

Mix all ingredients.

Finger Paint

2/3 cup elastic dry   1 cup Ivory Soap Flakes
  starch   oil of cloves, a few drops
1 cup cold water   (preservative) calcimine
3 cups boiling water   pigment, or vegetable coloring

Dissolve elastic starch in cold water. Smooth lumps and add boiling water. Stir constantly. Thicken but do not boil more than one minute. Add rest of ingredients (hot or cold). Use oil glazed paper, newsprint, or wrapping paper.

Sugar Flour Paste

1 cup flour	1 T. powdered alum
1 cup sugar	3 drops of oil of cloves
1 qt. water (2 cups cold, 2 cups hot)	

Mix flour and sugar together. Slowly stir in 1 cup of water. Bring remainder to boil and add the mixture to it, stirring constantly. Continue to cook and stir (30 minutes in a double broiler) until fairly clear. Remove from heat and add oil of cloves. Makes 1 quart of paste. Paste keeps a long time. Keep moist by adding small pieces of wet sponge to top of small jar of paste.

Bookbinder's Paste

1 tsp. flour	1/4 tsp. alum (powdered)
2 tsp. cornstarch	1/3 cup water

Mix dry ingredients. Add water slowly, stirring out lumps. Cook in a double boiler over low heat, stirring constantly. Remove from heat when paste begins to thicken; it will thicken more as it cools. Keep covered. Thin with water when necessary.

Sand Paint

1/2 cup sand (washed,   1 T. powder paint
   dried, and sifted)

Shake onto surface brushed with watered glue.

NOTE: Empty plastic vitamin or soap bubble bottles make excellent containers.

Soap Paint

1 1/2 cups soap flakes   1 cup hot or warm water

Whip with an eggbeater until stiff.

Play Dough Recipe

1 cup flour   1/2 cup salt
1 cup water   2 T. vanilla
1 T. oil   food coloring for desired
1 T. alum   intensity

Mix all dry ingredients. Add oil and water. Cook over medium heat, stirring constantly, until it reaches the consistency of mashed potatoes. Remove from heat and add vanilla and color. Divide into balls and work in color by kneading.

NOTE: This is a play dough recipe similar to the commercial type but more durable. Keep in a plastic bag or closed container when not being used.

 Blocks

Different children like different kinds of blocks: traditional hard wood blocks; oversized cardboard blocks; small plastic blocks like legos; or foam rubber blocks. Sometimes, children use all of them together for some really interesting looking structures.

Never forget that to kids, it's as much fun to unbuild as it is to build. Each shape and size block has a place on a shelf, and we always allow plenty of time to unbuild our structures. It's also a great way to learn about sorting.

We used to leave our structures up for several days, but lately—since we've gotten into unbuilding—we take them all down before everyone goes home. There's something exciting to the children about walking into the room in the morning and starting all over.

It is important to make sure that boys and girls have equal access to blocks. Sometimes the boys take them over, and the truth is, when girls begin using blocks, they like them every bit as much as the boys. You may have to structure time in a way to make sure everyone has equal access.

Blocks require very close supervision, especially when the buildings start getting really high. If wood blocks fall on a child, he can be hurt. Even the sound of a structure crashing can be alarming to a young child.

Chapter 6

BY THE BOOK

Maurice Sendak, the great writer-illustrator of children's books such as *Where the Wild Things Are* and *In the Night Kitchen*, has said, "As a child I felt that books were holy objects, to be caressed, rapturously sniffed, and devotedly provided for. I gave my life to them—I still do."

The rapture and joy that Sendak recalls from his childhood memories of reading can become a part of any child's life. Your work with young readers can make all the difference in getting them into a productive and lifelong reading habit. Here are some good ways to make that joy happen.

What Books Can Mean to a Child

Wholesome foods nourish a baby's body, and good books help their brains grow and learn. Read to a baby and you'll see that she laps up sounds, words, and pictures just as eagerly as she drinks her milk.

Some people think that reading to a baby is foolish and pressuring. Nothing could be further from the truth. Babies take readily to books, and those who learn to love them early in life have advantages in that they may become early readers. And early readers have a head start on language, a head start on thinking, and a head start on learning.

When to begin? Even before a baby can hold up his head, he can look at books and listen as you read aloud. Some parents read to babies even before they are born because research shows that babies really can hear voices from the world outside the womb.

If you have mixed age groups in your center, hold an infant on your lap, leaning against your chest right in front of the book, while toddlers cuddle up on each side. Everyone will be cozy and the infant will look at every page as you make your way through the book.

Reading to babies helps them learn patterns of sounds and rhythms of language long before actual words make sense to them. Toddlers also tune in to rhythms and repetitions, and may chime in on favorite lines as you read.

One of the obvious values of reading for children and adults alike is the vocabulary-building that results. Caregivers can foster this vocabulary-building by pointing to and identifying objects in the books they are reading.

For young children, books are all about looking and focusing attention. That's why they love books that involve finding things like *Where's Waldo?* by Martin Handford. You can turn any book into a "finding" book just by asking a question such as, "Where's the carrot on this page?"

Encourage parents to read to their children at home. If it's a home where you know there aren't many books, invite them to borrow a book for the night. Then make a big deal to the baby about how mommy and daddy are taking a special book home to share with her.

You don't have to be a great actor to read to a child. All you need is to modulate the sound of your voice so that it's pleasant to listen to. That, coupled with your pleasure in holding a child and your own interest in the story you're reading, is enough. Just find a time when both you and the baby are relaxed, pick a book you think you'll both like, hold the book so the baby can see the pictures, point to the familiar and unfamiliar objects on the page, and have fun!

Every interaction with a child has potential. When I change a diaper, I talk to the baby. When we're eating, we talk about the food. There is no such thing as "just maintenance" when you're working with kids. It's all about building trust.

If you really want to hone your skills as a story reader, listen to Jim Dale's audiotaped readings of the Harry Potter series. It's amazing how many different voices he can produce. You'll never match him so don't even bother to try, but you can get an idea for how to vary your voice and make your readings even more fun for the children.

Use the books you read with toddlers to kick off a conversation about their own lives. For instance, the wonderful story *Swimmy* by Leo Lionni can be a great occasion for talking about what it means to be different. *The Very Hungry Caterpillar* by Eric Carle can lead to conversation about how people grow, and how when everyone grows, they change.

Make sure you read books with infants, too. Margaret Wise Brown's books, *Goodnight Moon* and *The Runaway Bunny*, are great for that. They have the most wonderful rhythms and babies really get into them. Of course, you shouldn't ever worry about finishing a book, because babies rarely make it from cover to cover. In fact, they don't even know where the covers are!

If a baby wants to play with a toy while you read, let her. Don't worry about rules right now. You're trying to hook her on the love of reading, and maybe she'll love it more if she can play a little while she listens.

Story Time Means Lap Time

Whenever you can, hold children on your lap when you read to them. The intimacy of the reading experience and the quiet pleasure they get from reading will be reinforced by the coziness and warmth of a loving caregiver's lap.

If you're reading to a group of kids, let them cuddle in really close. Hold one of them on your lap for one book, another for another.

If a child digresses from a story you're reading to tell you a story of his own, let him digress. It's more important to listen to his story than it is to finish your book cover to cover.

When you read to babies, you're bringing the world right to their doors. What babies hear, see, and feel within the world of a book helps them make sense of the world. That's even more true as they get older. Books will help them to focus their eyes, learn more words, identify objects and ideas, distinguish sights and sounds, and stretch their imaginations.

Always check to make sure that the child you are reading to can see the pages. Reading at this point is as much a visual as an auditory experience.

When you know that the children you're reading to are very familiar with a book, try leaving out the last word of each page and let them fill it in. They'll be very proud of themselves.

Encourage children to bring their favorite book from home to share with their friends. Make sure that their names are written in it so it doesn't get mixed up with your library.

Even though the child you're reading to cannot read on her own, she still can turn pages. Inviting her to do so turns reading into a more meaningful, participatory experience.

When you're reading to very young children, they may turn the pages before you get to the end. Don't make a big deal of it. The actual story is much less important than their feeling of participation.

Young children often want to read a favorite page in a favorite book over and over. It seems strange to you to read the same page more than once because you're interested in advancing the plot. But for children, it's all about being with a familiar old friend. They like knowing what to expect. Don't bring your values to it. Learn to enjoy it from a child's point of view.

If you have a readily accessible library, preschoolers may pick up books to "read" on their own. Sometimes, their friends will gather around to listen to them read.

It's great to have a cozy, quiet place for kids to sit when they want to look at books. It's like a little haven for them.

Reading Do's and Don'ts

Don't set any arbitrary limits or goals. "Just two pages" or "only four pages" are not phrases that apply to book-time. A child's language development and love of reading will grow far more productively out of a warm cuddly time spent around one page than from a struggle to get to the end of the story.

Do try a few different short-story times (even one-minute ones) spaced through the day instead of one long story. They'll become moments everyone will look forward to, instead of moments that inspire fidgeting and fretting.

Don't try to turn books into pacifiers for fussy babies or rambunctious toddlers. Let a book do what it was conceived to do: entertain and stimulate a willing, alert, and interested child. If a book can help correct disruptive behavior, fine, but that's not it's reason for being.

Do set up a "library" in your space so that the covers of the books are on full display. Let your young readers pick out their favorites instead of always making the choice your own.

Do allow children to linger on a page. Reading is an experience that is meant to be savored. When a child wants to stay with a certain page, he is telling you that there is something delicious there, or something that he is trying to understand, or something that needs to be absorbed slowly. Allow a child that time and don't rush the process.

Do allow children to read the same book over and over again. Writer/critic Nancy Spain once said, "I only really love a book when I have read it four times." That's the way children feel about books they love; they want to go back to them continually. That insistence is tied closely to the love of reading, and should be indulged good-naturedly and even encouraged.

Don't allow a child to do something to a book that you wouldn't do to a book. That means no throwing of books, no chewing on books, and no ripping of books. If any of that behavior occurs, firmly but gently end the story time and go on to another activity. And you can say, "Books are for reading."

Do let preschoolers help you mend books that may be torn. They'll feel good about helping an old friend.

Don't punish children around reading time. If a toddler becomes bored during story time, don't put him in "time out" for his lack of attention. Focus him on some alternate activity while you finish up with the others.

Do encourage toddlers to create their own "books." Little stories can become exciting works of literature in these young creative hands. All it requires is some construction paper, crayons, and a stapler!

Become the Best Kind of Reader You Can Be

The more you can become an engaging performer, the more you will engage the children who are your audience. That means using your voice as a tool that will make the reading exciting, or gestures to emphasize important points. Don't be shy. Banish the monotone and bring on the dramatics!

It's great to use puppets or props to help tell a story. This is an especially great technique to hold on to children who tend to wander about or fidget.

As with all the other activities you do with your children, reading to them works better when you have a clear understanding of the developmental stages of childhood. Expecting rapt attention from a child who is developmentally unable to give you that attention is frustrating for reader and readee alike!

Let children read to you. Preschoolers probably know their favorite books by heart. If you've been an expressive reader for them, they'll be an expressive reader right back.

Never correct a child when she's reading to you, even if the words she's saying have nothing to do with the book she's reading from.

Choosing and Caring for Books

Some books are better than others. And some books are better than just about anything! Train yourself to become a discerning critic when it comes to books. The input of your young readers—their interest level, their engagement, and their enthusiasm—will serve as a useful touchstone. Also, when choosing books, consider the following points.

Some books have unusual or even gimmicky features such as things to pull, things to slide, and other "hands on" activities. These can be great fun, but first must be checked to make sure they are safe, and that there are no small parts or sharp corners that might hurt little hands.

Paperback books last forever if you put clear contact paper on the front and back covers.

Pop-up books are very fragile. Does anyone have an intact copy of *Pat the Bunny* for more than a year? They're better off kept at home.

Always ask a child what book he'd like to read. If you've got a group that is going to argue over your selection, make it yourself but keep their favorites in mind.

Whenever your center gets new books, introduce them to the children the way you would introduce a new friend. Make a big deal about it. They'll come to understand that books make *great* gifts.

Suggest to parents that they donate a book to the center each year in honor of their child's birthday. It's a great way to build up your library and a really nice way to make children feel important.

Children will enjoy books most that in some way connect with their life experiences. Animals, families, games, dolls, holidays, trees, the beach: these and many more will be particularly meaningful subjects for the young reader.

Nothing brings more pleasure than clear, beautiful, unusual, and appealing illustrations. Books don't need lots of lavish illustrations in bright colors, but early readers do look for those visual ingredients to break up the words.

Always be aware of the reading level of the book you're planning to share with your children. If the book has words, are they short and simple? Are the sentences easy to understand? What about the story? Can it be easily followed? In good children's books, pictures and text work together to promote comprehension. How do the pictures and texts fit together in the book you've chosen to read?

Many children enjoy having their reality reinforced with simple books about simple, everyday things. But reading is also a good opportunity to explore the fantasies of a child's inner life with non-threatening pictures and texts. Reading fantasy books can spin off into picture-drawing, dress-up, and other fantasy-filled activities.

All reading facilitates learning, but one of the particular values of certain reading experiences is that it can help a young child learn about the many different kinds of people in the world and their diverse cultures, religions, ages, and appearances. Does the book you've chosen help break down cultural barriers or does it present stereotypes that would be better avoided?

There are some books out there that specifically promote values and character-building. This can be valuable, but many books do just that without addressing that purpose so overtly. Read between the lines of your book to determine what kind of values are being written about. Then ask yourself if the book reflects the kind of values you want the children in your care to develop with regard to gender roles, relationships, and violence.

Children can be tough audiences.
Sometimes, a book has to "grab" them from the start. Does the book you're planning to read have the power to do that? If not, you might want to use some kind of prop to reinforce the book's message and grab attention such as a puppet, a bubble blower, a kazoo, or a crystal, any and all of which might be used to underline some theme or character in the book.

Board books are very durable and make it easy for very young page-turners to get those pages turned.

Never bother with books that you find really boring. The more enthusiastic you are about what you're reading, the more enthusiastic will be the children. They know when you're faking it!

Some people buy plastic books that become bathtub toys, but books are books and boats are boats. It's fine for children to learn the difference early on.

Encourage parents to sit down and read a book when they drop their child off in the morning, or if they're rushed, at the end of the day. It's a great way to connect with your child's parents.

Some children like to take a book with them to the potty or to their cots at nap time. Those are great habits to establish early in life. Going to sleep with a book is like going to sleep with a special lovey.

A Starter Set of Great Books for Young Readers

Clap Hands by Helen Oxenbury

Farm Noises by Jane Miller

The Chicken Book by Garth Williams

Rosie's Walk by Pat Hutchins

Freight Train by Donald Crews

Goodnight Moon by Margaret Wise Brown

The Runaway Bunny by Margaret Wise Brown

I Went Walking by Sue Williams

Lap-time Song and Play Book compiled by Jane Yolen

Chapter 7

THE LEARNING CURVE

aregivers and parents alike often ask themselves how much they should be teaching their very young children. In today's fasttrack world, there is much pressure to give children a "head start." There are companies that make flashcards for newborns; and there are special recordings that are supposed to boost a child's IQ if you begin playing them while you're pregnant.

The bottom line is that babies are *always* learning, and they are learning from everything around them. The most important kind of learning takes place when we create rich environments, and share our lives with babies in an open, caring way. For little ones, learning is an organic process. They keep their eyes open. They listen. Their brains are like little sponges. And, most important, they are driven to learn. The desire and ability to learn comes pro-grammed in at birth.

When we buy into the external pressure to "teach" babies, and start drilling them with flash-cards and the like, we actually are interfering with their natural drive to learn. This chapter will draw on the experience of child care providers, and explore the many fun and healthy ways that caregivers can facilitate the incredible natural way in which young children learn.

Infants: Routines and Explorations

An infant's day revolves around such caregiving activities as feeding, diapering, and being held. It is amazing how much infants learn in the context of these routines. As you change an infant or feed him, you can foster his language development by talking to him. Your facial expressions will become his guideposts in learning how he can impact others with his actions. When you smile and softly touch an infant, you are teaching him early lessons in self-esteem and trust. Everything you do with regard to an infant is a kind of teaching because every experi-ence for an infant is about learning.

Playing with objects is another important way that infants learn. That's why archaeologists have found baby rattles dating back to Egyptian times. The need for such stimuli always has been recognized. When babies are awake and alert, they need the right stuff—equipment, materials, and activities—to encourage exploration. This "stuff" doesn't need to be expensive or designed by scientists. It does, however, need to be safe.

To provide effectively what babies need, you as a caregiver will have to be attuned to the "work" that a baby is doing at any given time. That means becoming an observer and teaching yourself about the stages of development that a child goes through. You'll want to have some sense of what it means when a baby puts her hands into her mouth or plays with her feet. And then you'll want to give her the right "tools" to do her "work." Keep in mind, however, that each baby is unique. Two babies of the same age may be at very different stages of development. No value judgments should be ascribed to one or the other. Instead, support each baby as best you can.

Your success as a facilitator of valuable play will be dependent, to a large extent, on the imagination and knowledge you bring to the table. The following ideas, gathered from child care workers, can be adapted for your own use or may inspire some new ideas.

Let's say you have a baby in your room who loves to tap a spoon against his high chair tray, his bowl, his cup, or anywhere else he can. He is learning about the world through his rich auditory experiences. You can make these experiences even richer by giving him more opportunities to experiment with sound. That means hollow things, metal things that give off a deep rich gong, squeaky things, and so on. You can help his language skills along by teaching words that underscore the sounds he is hearing such as "Bang!" "Bong!" "Tap-Tap." "Tom-Tom."

Another baby in your room is also into metal bowls, but more for the cool, hard way they feel than the sounds she can make with them. This baby is into a tactile experience of the world and would surely appreciate more items of varied texture. Watch how excited she gets by experimenting with a piece of sticky tape, a scrap of velvet, fake fur, or some sandpaper. Again, you'll want to reinforce her experience with language, using the words "sticky," "scratchy," "soft," "fuzzy" to create a vocabulary for her.

You can make a "touch cube" by covering the six sides of a cardboard box with different textures: sandpaper, velvet, plush carpet, mylar, double-sided sticky tape, or cork. *Caution:* Make certain that none of the coverings can be removed by the baby.

You really need to think about infants in terms of different learning styles. Some infants love to be in the middle of lots of action and noise. Others tune out or get anxious when there is too much going on. Make sure you give each child what he or she needs.

When you feel like an infant is starting to tune out—to turn his eyes away from you, for example—it means he's had enough and needs some downtime.

Consider the situation of a slightly older baby who is working on coordinating the muscles in her arms and legs. She is climbing up your step stool which is not such a good idea. You have to meet her need by becoming inventive and developing an "exerciser" that is safe and sufficiently challenging. Get crafty and create a safe, low climber. By low, we mean no higher than 24 inches. A ramp made from sturdy cardboard or boards would do nicely. Make sure that the edges are well-padded with foam or fabric. When the little climber has mastered the task of going up and down the ramp, hike up the angle of the board and then throw down the gauntlet. "Can you get up that ramp?" you challenge. "Can you get down?" Watch and support her as she solves the problem, making sure to intercept only if frustration or fatigue threatens to overcome her.

It's great to have a full-zone climbing apparatus of at least four feet with a mat below for safety's sake.

As a rule, don't rush in to "save" infants from their problems. You need to walk that fine line between allowing them enough frustration to make the next step, but not allowing so much frustration as to make them give up.

Keep in mind that infants put everything in their mouths. It's one of their most accurate ways of exploring an object. They don't yet have the hand control to explore with their fingers, and they can't really steady a toy at a comfortable distance in front of their eyes. But they're geniuses when it comes to tonguing things. Make sure everything is clean and smooth so they can get to work.

Nobody is objecting to ready-made toys. They make our lives easier, and many of them are far better designed and pass more stringent safety tests than anything we could come up with on our own. But sometimes, as a caregiver, you will find yourself in a position where you need to "customize" a toy for a child who needs that certain stimulation he's looking for. For instance, if a child is trying to fit shapes into a sorting ball, but the spaces are too small for him and he's getting frustrated, that means he needs something less challenging. You come to the rescue with your home-made shoe box sorter. You've cut holes into the top, and for pegs you use something smooth-edged, easy to handle, and too big to choke on. You reinforce self-esteem by praising each small victory. Then, when he's ready for a bigger challenge, you up the ante by lining the openings with foam rubber that provides some resistance so he really has to push hard to get the pegs through. Clever child. Clever you!

Safety First

A toy is only as good as it is safe. Safety is the number one criterion in picking out play materials. How do you establish the safety of any given item? Here are some tips.

o   Look the item over carefully to start with.

o   Make sure that you do not give a toy to an infant if the toy is less than $1\frac{5}{8}$" in diameter.

o   Invest in one of those little choke-testers. They are plastic tubes into which you put a toy. If the toy comes out the other end, then it is too small for a baby to play with.

o   Use only toys and materials that can be sanitized easily.

o   Small pieces and sharp edges are a no-no. Again, inspect carefully.

o   Continually check wooden toys to make sure they have not developed any splintered surfaces.

o   Some materials, such as paint or styrofoam, erode over time, and can flake or crumble when they are mouthed or chewed. Inspect for such wear.

o   Don't use old or antique painted toys. They may be painted with lead paint.

o   Never use a balloon as a toy. Children have died from suffocation after inhaling a fragment of a popped balloon.

Toddlers (12 Months and Older): Active Explorers

When dealing with toddlers, the first question that you, as a caregiver, will find yourself asking is just how much can those little brains actually hold? And, based on that answer, your next question will probably be What should I be teaching?

The answer to the first question is that those little brains can hold a lot! The toddlers who come to you are poised at that pivotal moment in life when they first start to understand that certain symbols stand for certain objects and things. We call this symbolic representation. For example, Molly now understands that a photograph of Grandma is not the same as Grandma herself, but is a *symbol* of her.

Once that sense of symbolic representation kicks in, toddlers can begin to have fun playing with these symbols. For instance, a toddler might engage in pretend play by picking up a telephone and having a conversation with mommy. This kind of simple symbolic play may develop into extended fantasy play as the child grows older.

Cognitively speaking, the toddler's emerging ability to engage in symbolic thought and play depends on the development of multisensory areas of the brain located in the frontal, parietal, and temporal lobes. These areas develop slowly, but once the toddler has his symbolic thought processes nailed down, he should begin, sometime in his second year, to put those symbolic thought processes on the back burner while he attends to more basic sensory and motor experiences such as climbing, swinging, pouring water from jugs at water play, or sifting sand at the sand table.

When toddlers are immersed in the world of sensory and motor experiences, they learn best through "hands-on" experiences. They will want to experiment with a whole bunch of materials that speak to their senses. Telling them that the way to produce the color purple is by mixing red and blue together is not going to work as well as giving them red and blue paint and inviting them to experiment. In other words, "teaching" a toddler at this stage is most effective when that teaching is aimed at "facilitating" her own discoveries.

Toddlers also spend lots of time engaged in the act of remembering things. The names of teachers and other children, books they love, and games they play are the tasks of the day. This whole process happens naturally. You don't want to quiz toddlers and make them anxious about learning because they are the epitome of the self-directed learner. An excellent way to boost the memory retention of toddlers is by incorporating music into the learning arena. For reasons that no one fully understands yet, musical rhythms help to lodge words and information in the minds of young children.

Speaking of these young minds, just how retentive are they? Research shows that toddlers have fairly well-developed, short-term memories, but they lack a real sense of time. For instance, it is difficult for a toddler to remember when a particular event actually happened. Was it yesterday? The day before that? A month ago? Sam can vividly remember the high-wire artists from the circus he attended, but he can't remember exactly when he was there. This memory lag probably has to do with the slow maturation of the hippocampus, the area of the brain located in the temporal lobes, that rules memory. Before long, however, memory in most toddlers will get up to speed and it becomes time for a more structured kind of learning. It is not something you need to help them with. It is a developmental process that will unfold on its own.

Here are some tips from other child care workers about what you can do to help your toddlers make the most of this challenging and exciting period of their cognitive development.

Create a secure and supportive environment in which your toddlers will feel safe to explore. This means not only a learning field that is free of physical stumbling blocks and pitfalls, but also one in which a child can feel that she will not be laughed at, harshly criticized, or suffocated with overprotection.

Make sure the toddlers and preschoolers see you having lots of positive interactions with their parents. Talk to them by name. Welcome them every morning at the same time you welcome the child. That makes the child feel safe, and when he feels safe, he's open to learning.

You can tell a lot from a room as soon as you walk into it. If you want to create a room that's going to encourage learning you need to:

o   hang lots of wonderful pictures on the wall.

o   make sure there are pictures at eye level of a crawler.

o   create different and defined areas of interest.

o   art, dress-up, music, fine motor, gross motor, science/sensory, blocks and building, language/ listening, and so on.

o   have lots of color and light, and objects that will delight a baby's eyes, ears, nose, and little fingers.

o   offer opportunities for sand and water play.

o   have a good supply of craft materials like play-dough and fingerpaints.

o   have lots of fun props like fake food and cooking implements.

o   offer opportunities for dress-up and fantasy play with plenty of adult clothing, dolls, blocks, and toy vehicles.

Avoid the teaching of specific academic skills like number-learning, alphabets, colors, and shapes. They'll learn those things naturally in the course of their activities. If parents or grandparents are worried that you don't stress academics, explain to them that babies learn best from doing the things they love in a very natural way. For instance, it is best to teach colors by asking children at lunch whether they would prefer a red or a green apple. Would they like one, two, or three raisins? Get the idea?

Learning is best undertaken in an atmosphere of sharing and good will. Make sure you model positive behavior for your children by the way you interact with them, their parents, and other staff members.

Cognition and Learning

If a baby keeps dropping a little stuffed bear to the floor over and over and over again, do you regard it as his personal campaign to drive you insane? If so, you don't understand what's actually going on here. Yes, babies engage in repetitive behavior and, yes, it can seem absolutely maddening at times, but they do so with no malice aforethought. What is happening here is a case of "practice makes perfect."

Practice is critical for children who are mastering their motor skills. That's why babies push the same red button on the toy cash register over and over again. In much the same way, the repeated "experiments" that babies perform with objects and people are just as critical a form of practice. This kind of practice helps babies master what they need to know about their physical and social environments. For instance, when a baby wants to play a peek-a-boo game over and over and over again—way beyond the limits of all adult endurance—she wants to do so for a reason. What she is learning is object permanence, or, otherwise put, the fact that something doesn't disappear just because she can't see it.

Similarly, when Scottie keeps dropping his little bear to the floor, he's not just finding out about the limits of your patience; he's learning about gravity, or cause and effect. Like motor skills, reasoning does best with practice and repetition. It's a way to help reasoning "sink in."

When it comes to repetition and practice, some parents and caregivers assume that practicing facts with flashcards will help a baby's brain develop more quickly. The truth is, however, that there is no research to support this assumption. Flashcards can, in fact, slow a baby's learning because she may resent the tedium of it. Infants and toddlers do their best learning when they are invited and encouraged to use all their senses, and to explore their environment thoroughly. That means lots of touching, smelling, squeezing, poking, tasting, and manipulating objects (and, up to a point, people too!). This kind of exploratory play provides all the stimulation that a developing brain needs. So put the flashcards on the tag sale pile and focus in on these good ideas instead.

Use the real thing instead of flashcards. Point to your own nose and say "nose," your own eyes and say "eyes," baby's foot and say "foot." All of those are far more memorable and evocative than any flashcard ever could be.

Whenever a baby points to something, give her the words to describe it. "That's the ball. Would Lucy like the ball?"

When you see babies expressing feelings like great happiness or sadness, give them those words also. "Sally looks very sad." "Is Jaime lonely and missing his mommy?" Children who have words to describe emotions have a much easier time, as they get older, handling those emotions.

Remember what we just said about touching, smelling, squeezing, poking, tasting, and manipulating objects? And let's not forget banging, bouncing, stretching, and lots of other ways to explore. Make sure that the environment you invite children into every day has plenty of opportunities for all of the above. Remember that probably everything will go into a child's mouth at some point or other, so it must be safe and clean.

Resign from the "No Mess Police." If you have a major problem with mess, you've probably found yourself in the wrong line of work and will want to retool for something neat like banking. Look mess in the eye and learn to love it. It's creativity! And don't forget that once upon a time, you were a messy little person, too, exploring your pasta bowl with your greasy little fingers and making mush of a ripe banana.

Inside that messy child may lie a sense of order waiting to get out. That means that most children, when they're not smearing fingerpaint into their hair, like to do things like put stuff from one container into another, or fill up a pail, dump it, and fill it up again. That quest for order is one way that a child has of feeling that he can control his environment. That kind of control takes a lot of practice, so be prepared to fill up that pail over and over and over again.

If you subscribe to the belief that some mess is good, but are also of the belief that there is a limit to all good things, there are ways that you can control mess without inhibiting exploration. For instance, if you think a child would enjoy experimenting with the experience of feeling a squishy substance but you don't want that squish all over the place, try putting the questionable substance into a Zip-Lock® bag. A lump of Jell-O®, for instance, can be fun to manipulate, but Jell-O® all over the place might not be so much fun. Little is lost in the translation, however, when you contain the quivery delight inside a bag that you then offer up for a "Feel Me" game. Make sure, however, that your little explorer doesn't bite through and chew the bag.

There is no shortage of wonderfully colorful and creative board books out there whose purpose for babies is to reinforce both the symbology for familiar objects (hat, bed, doll, umbrella) and to introduce them to things not in their immediate environment (elephant, mountain, train). Many of these board books are so engaging that kids soon will memorize them and think that they are "reading" along.

Curriculum and the Child Care Center

Speaking of "reading," does a preschool curriculum for toddlers make sense altogether? We spoke about the pitfalls of pressure, but many parents and other significant adults are anxious to increase their children's brain capacity and give them a head start in their learning. What's the right answer?

To begin with, the word "curriculum" simply means a plan for learning. And any plan for learning should begin with one basic building block: a positive, supportive environment. Such an environment will help your toddlers achieve optimal brain growth and develop skills in all areas of cognition.

To create a positive, supportive learning environment, we have to think about what kind of a curriculum makes sense for toddlers. We know that children this age can be quite capable learners. We also know that a child's experiences during the early years can be crucial in forming a solid foundation for future learning. How then can we best enable toddlers to maximize their learning and achieve that solid foundation?

When curriculum planning comes to mind, the kind of development that most of us tend to envision is intellectual in nature. With toddlers, however, you cannot separate out intellectual needs. Any educational curriculum devised for toddlers should be essentially a joining together of all a toddler's needs: physical, social, emotional, cognitive, and linguistic.

As we suggested above, the best way to stimulate a toddler's thinking processes is to focus on the day-to-day interactions and routines that are the stuff of his world in and around the child care center. What makes for a good toddler curriculum? It is all the daily routines that she comes to know—nap time, lunch, snack, toilet time, song time, story circle, outdoor time—and all the problems, challenges, solutions, and victories that come out of those. In other words, while the daily routines are going on, so are all the skill-building that accompanies them, whether it be conversation, gross-motor activities like climbing and running, fine-motor activities like buttoning and tieing, social interaction, cooperative learning, problem-solving with peers, and so much more.

Looked at that way, curriculum development for toddlers dovetails precisely with what you do with them anyway on a day-to-day basis. So feel free to think of yourself as a developer of curriculum, and take into account some of these specific tips that might help you in that work.

First and always, you must recognize that learning occurs most successfully in an environment where a child feels safe and valued. One way to promote that feeling is to maintain a beneficial caregiver-child ratio. Another important point to keep in mind is that children have the need to form special attachments and it is very good for them to bond with a particular individual. Encourage caregivers to let themselves form special bonds. Usually, everyone finds someone special. If one child seems to be having a problem forming a special bond, it's a good thing to talk about at staff meetings.

Play is a child's work. Make sure you incorporate liberal amounts of play time throughout the day. Ensure that your space is conducive to safe and expansive play, and that the appropriate materials are on hand.

Study the play habits of your children. Be involved but not overly involved. There are appropriate times to step in and appropriate times to step back. The more you observe play, the more you will develop a natural sense of what your role should be in any given situation.

If you see a group of toddlers preparing a make-believe meal, you might sit down and ask for a taste of what they're cooking. Then tell them how yummy it is. Let them lead while you follow.

Provide *scaffolding*. The concept of scaffolding involves the fostering of independence and autonomy in a child, but also stepping in to help—to lend the scaffold—as needed. Children can become frustrated quickly by problems that overly tax their

developing problem-solving skills, and you will want
to intercept them before that frustration makes them
give up.

Become a record-keeper. Even if you don't
like to write, you still can jot down brief notes, perhaps as little as a sentence a day, on a child's behavior
and play style. Be objective. This will provide a base-
line by which you can gauge a child's progress or
regression. It is also something you can share mean-
ingfully with a parent in a conference.

Make sure to tell parents whenever a child
learns something new. For one thing, it makes them
feel included. For another, it deepens the bond
between you. Whenever you deepen that bond, the
baby is the big winner.

Chapter 8

Getting Along and Staying Well

A child care center, like a family, can be full of love and full of conflict at the same time. For most children, the center becomes a training ground where one can learn valuable lessons about relationships. Many families, struggling with the demands of raising children in a modern world where time is short and pressure is high, come to see the center as a kind of net. In the very best situations, everyone is connected—teacher to child; teacher to parent; child to child; parent to parent; and parents to other children—and these connections offer a unique foundation that the child can build on for the rest of his life. But nets, sturdy as they are, must be maintained and repaired when worn.

Another way in which a child care center is like a family involves the sharing of all kinds of bugs and germs. One day one baby has a stomach flu, and the next day half the baby room is out sick. And the generosity doesn't end there. Child care workers, like moms and dads, spend their time in intimate contact with their tiny charges, being sneezed on, breathed on, drooled on, hugged, kissed, and more.

Here are thoughts on how we can keep our nets in good shape and our bodies in good health.

Making Friends

Some people are skeptical when it comes to the idea of young children forming real friendships. They've obviously never spent much time around a child care center. If you're a caregiver, then surely you've witnessed the caring and affection that can go on even among the youngest children. But it takes work, thought, and insight to set the stage for good relationships between and among little ones. Here are some tips on how to make that aspect of your center as strong as it can be.

Set up a buddy system in your room. It's a good way to build connections. The buddies can be changed by the day or the week, whatever works. A buddy group or "team" can be fun, too. The Red Tomatoes or the White Mice, for instance, with name-tags, "meetings," and things like that. It's a nice way to have everyone discover each other!

Children learn about positive relationships from what they see around them. That means that you, as a caregiver, need to model positive, prosocial behavior with your fellow teachers, with parents, and, of course, with the children. That means no yelling, no demeaning words, and no cold shoulders!

Build on the positive. If friendships in the room fray, don't look for culprits. Just tell yourself that children of this age are not models of consistency. When they are being good friends to each other, comment and commend. When they're not being good friends to each other, say as little as you can get away with.

Always make room for special relationships that develop between specific caregivers and children. These special relationships don't mean that other children are neglected. They're just a natural part of the way people connect, and most kids develop those relationships at some point or other.

Preschoolers can sometimes intentionally exclude each other when they're playing. Vivian Paley, renowned educator, wrote a book entitled *You Can't Say You Can't Play*. It was a simple rule in her kindergarten classroom at the University of Chicago Lab School. She talked about it with the kids at length. They had wonderful discussions. But, ultimately, school was a place where that rule was enforced, and in a very short time everyone came to accept it. The younger the children are when you make this rule, the more natural it will feel.

Mine! Mine! Mine!

If you work with children, the "mine" word is right up there in the top ten, along with bottle, juice, and bye-bye. *Mine* signifies the conflict a young child feels about sharing. Sharing is an important concept for children to master, but they aren't really ready to understand it until they're approaching their fourth birthday. You can teach about turn-taking and you can make certain that the idea of turn-taking is enforced in a fair way, but the spirit of really "sharing" is not something you can expect from very young children.

Let's have a look at some of the issues around sharing and how different caregivers handle them.

What's the Problem?   Children who have a hard time sharing should not be viewed as "problem" children. They are not being bad or even selfish. They simply are responding appropriately to developmental signals and need to grow a little. You can help them find the resources to do that.

Developmentally speaking, toddlers between the ages of 18 to 24 months are experimenting with a new awareness of self. That means that not only is there a "me" but also a "mine." And the "mine" is an extension of the "me." Therefore, Johnny's ball and Johnny himself tend to get all wrapped up together in Johnny's mind.

Mine is also a way for Johnny to stake out the world. At this age, he's like a little conqueror. The more he gets, the bigger he feels. The bigger he feels, the safer he thinks he is. Sometimes, this leads to a compulsion to possess things, as toddlers go around a room claiming what they want for themselves. This drive to get lots of stuff is also a way for them to say, "Look at me. Look at me."

Toddlers at this age also tend to be extremely shaky around the issue of self-control. And self-control is a necessary component in the two-way tango that makes for good sharing. Bethany can wait a second or two, or maybe even three, while Maggie is playing with the monkey sock doll. But then she wants it! And, unable to control herself any longer, she reaches out and grabs it, setting off a flash fire of conflict. The kind of self-control we're talking about will kick in eventually, further along the developmental time line, as the brain matures. The fact that Bethany grabs the doll from Maggie when she is two doesn't mean she'll be grabbing things from kids when she is six. In fact, many people believe that children who are very confident about getting what they want, and who aren't forced to share before they are developmentally ready to, will end up being more relaxed about sharing in the years ahead.

Of course, sharing toys at a child care center is a different issue than sharing toys at home. At a child care center, the toys don't belong to any single child. They are there to be used by everyone. That's why dealing with issues around sharing is a big part of a caregiver's job. Here are some tips that will help you negotiate this area successfully.

Caregivers need to have a good grasp of child development. That means knowing where a child is at any given time in his physical, intellectual, and emotional growth. If you understand development, the expectations you bring to a situation will more likely jibe with the reality.

Initiate and model games of sharing. Something simple like "Red Light, Green Light" can become a demonstration of turn-taking and appropriate sharing behavior.

A child who brings a special toy from home is not going to want to share that toy with anyone else. It's as simple as that. All the children at the center should have an awareness of the specialness of certain toys. These toys can be presented and "shared" in a formal circumstance, like circle time, but then they should be stored in a private, secure place—like a cubby—so that the child doesn't have to worry about anyone taking what is his.

If you notice that a certain toy is very popular—let's say a soft squishy ball or a fireman's hat—try to have multiples on hand. This reduces the opportunities for conflict over sharing and makes everyone's life easier.

It should be understood that toddlers, who often are less than willing to share in the best of circumstances, become even less compliant when they are tired or not feeling well. Allow children who are feeling *low-energy* to have extra space.

Never make a child apologize for being unwilling to share. The apology is meaningless. And it's not great for toddlers to learn to say things they don't really mean.

Make sure that toddlers who are taking turns with a toy are closely supervised. It helps them stay in control when they know there is a teacher nearby to help them.

Kitchen timers are great mediators when it comes to sharing. When that nice loud bell goes off, it is time to pass the toy to a friend.

Always acknowledge how difficult it is for children to pass toys to a friend before they really want to. There's nothing wrong with that feeling, and it helps them to hear you say, "I know it's hard to stop playing with that doll right now but very soon it will be your turn again."

While a child is waiting his turn to play with something, it's a good idea to distract him with something else. Make sure you have plenty of things available for that purpose.

Curbing Aggressive Behavior

Between the ages of two and three, all kinds of conflicts can trigger what looks like aggressive behavior. If Sally has a truck that Joey wants, she might clobber him over the head and pull it out of his hands. If Sammy races with Alice, and Alice wins and says, "I won," he may push her down. And if three kids decide to tease a fourth, he may not say a word until a fifth child walks over and then vents all of his anger on her.

How do you handle aggressive behavior in a child care setting? All child care providers would agree that it simply cannot be tolerated, but different people deal with it in different ways.

You have to understand where the child is developmentally to deal with aggressive behavior effectively. Children of this age are experimenting with their sense of self. That's why they're always saying, Mine! Mine! These toddlers and preschoolers love to be with their friends, but they're primarily looking out for Number 1. They aren't able yet to think about other kids' feelings, especially when they're feeling their own so strongly. It is something they need to be taught in a loving way. First, you need to acknowledge their feelings, and then tell them about the other child's feelings. "I see that you're angry, but you cannot hurt Joey. Now Joey is hurting and I won't let anyone hurt anyone else when they're here."

It's important that the child who has been hurt also speak. You never want to create a situation where a child feels like a victim. If the kid who's been hurt looks the other child in the face and says, "You hurt me," it makes a big difference. You can be there to help make him feel safe, but he needs to say the words.

When you force young children to apologize, they end up feeling humiliated. If you make it clear that they've hurt someone and that you under-stand how intense their feelings were, you can tell them to think about it. And you can suggest that if they feel sorry, they can tell that to the child they hurt. We tell them that they can express their sorry feelings later if they want to, and you'd be surprised how often they do it on their own. That's when it's meaningful.

For young children, emotions are very fluid. They might be feeling ecstatically happy one moment and be crying the next. They have so many emotions near the surface that it's easy for them to erupt. Frustration can turn into anger like a flash fire, and if someone is in the way, it can be dangerous. That's why whenever groups are together, a caretaker needs to supervise closely.

The key is to step in *before* kids become aggressive and model the kind of behavior you want to see. You might say, "Everyone wants to play with the same ball. Does anyone have a solution?" Once it's in their court, they can actually talk about what to do with each other, with your guidance.

There's a huge variation of verbal ability among preschoolers. Usually, the children who have the easiest time expressing themselves verbally have less frustration to deal with and are less likely to hit.

Because of these developmental differences in language acquisition, it is very important for you, as a caregiver, to pay careful attention to a toddler's non-verbal cues so that you can help him connect the words with the feelings and actions.

Shame rears its ugly head, as does anxiety, pride, joy, and many more emotions that the children cannot begin to understand, anticipate, or deal with effectively. Fortunately, you are there to help them. One way you can do this is by labeling their feelings, making room for them, and assuring them that whatever they are feeling is all right to feel. But a feeling is one thing. A push, a shove, or a pinch is quite another.

Give them lots of room to move, run, and jump. Sometimes, children get aggressive with each other because they simply need to move. Toddlers need lots of space. If you don't have it indoors, make sure to get them outside as often as possible, all year long, even if that means mittens and boots and hats and winter jackets.

Some preschoolers like to pretend-fight. Different caregivers have different levels of tolerance for this kind of play. There is nothing wrong with it and, in fact, it's a great way to keep the distinction between fighting and not-really-fighting. The problem is that it doesn't always take much for a pretend-fight to turn into a real fight. If you're comfortable with this kind of play, you need to supervise it very closely and make a clear announcement about when it is over.

Use Your Words

It is never too early to start teaching the children in your care to use words. Even if their entire vocabulary amounts to one word—NO! for instance—that is vastly preferable to a punch, a kick, or a bite. If a two-year old takes a cookie from the hand of his friend, and the friend says "NO!" you can amplify for them. "Sounds to me like Sarah is very angry that you took her cookie. Why don't you give it back to her and ask me for a cookie? I'd be glad to give you one of your own."

It's always good to model using language about feelings when you're with kids. If a child does something nice for you, make it a point to say, "You are such a loving person. It makes me feel good just to be with you." And if a child acts aggressively, you can say, "I don't like being with you when you try to hurt me." The more you do that, the easier it is for kids to associate words with those feelings and behaviors.

Impulse control comes with the maturation of thinking skills. It cannot be rushed. It can, however, be supported, as you use your words to help them learn words of their own by which to frame their thoughts. Impulse control occurs in several stages. First, children have to know the rule ("There is no grabbing of objects here, Terry"). Then you can direct the rule to the actual situation at hand ("Terry, you grabbed the car out of Matthew's hand. You know that's not allowed."). Finally, you can direct them to the appropriate behavior by offering alternatives ("There is another truck on the shelf behind you, Terry. Why don't you play with that one until Matthew is finished?"). Over time, the children will internalize your directions and hear your words in their heads.

Sometimes less is more. In other words, a lot of words can sometimes add up to fewer results. Keep your words focused and effective. For instance, you might watch Terry out of the corner of your eye, knowing that he sees himself as a conqueror these days, and, with your well-chosen words, you might be able to head him off at the pass. "Terry," you would say, "do you want to play with Matthew? I see another car on the shelf behind you."

One part of your role as caregiver is to be the mediator between warring parties. It goes with the territory. Be fair and direct when you guide toddler behavior. Make decisions and stick with them.

Be clear in the way you express yourself. "When Matthew is finished, it will be your turn, Terry." Clear and simple. "Your turn is almost up, Matthew. Then it's Terry's turn." Clear and simple.

To help a child control her aggressive behavior, you will want to offer a variety of coping strategies and alternatives to that behavior. Get creative! For instance, you might have a Cool-Out Corner where a child can go when things are getting too hot. You can make it fun by putting a stuffed penguin in there and pictures of polar bears, seals, and other animals from frigid climates. The big inflatable doll that children can knock over when they need to let off steam is always a reliable standby. Or how about a Counting Corner where a child can learn to count to ten, filled with multiples of different objects such as balls, beanbags, and the like?

Children need to understand that aggressive behavior carries consequences. Again, clearly and simply state the consequences so there is as little confusion as possible. For example, you might say, "Terry, if you try to take the car away from Matthew again without asking him, you will have to leave the play area." And make sure you follow through. Idle threats are a very bad idea!

Avoid labeling the children in your care. It may be a natural impulse to do so, but just because it's natural doesn't mean it's constructive. Also, if you have a good overview of developmental issues, you will know that the child whom you are thinking of as "bad" is actually a child who is just at a less evolved place developmentally, and who is having a hard time keeping up with the demands of being in a community. Weed out words like "good," "bad," "cooperative," "uncooperative," "sweet," and "mean" from your vocabulary. They serve little, if any, purpose.

When redirecting a child who has been acting out, do your best to show that you still value her. "I love you, Cindy," you might say, "but I don't love the way you're acting right now." And reinforce positive behavior as much as you can. "It's so nice how you're sharing, Cindy. You've gotten so good at sharing."

Schedule parent meetings to talk about the way you deal with aggressive behavior at your center. It is important for parents to know, for example, that you shouldn't force children to apologize which some parents may do out of embarrassment.

If you notice one child getting into a lot of fights, call the parents in to talk about it. This should not be an "Uh-oh-is-he-in-trouble meeting." It should be a "Lets-see-what-we-can-do-to-help-Matthew meeting."

Conflict Resolution

It's great when you can curb aggressive behavior before it gets out of hand, but you're not Superman and you won't always be able to do that. Here, then, are some tips on how to handle conflict when it breaks out so that everybody can come out feeling like a winner.

Conflict between very young children often comes like a flash flood. It arrives without warning and everybody, including you the caregiver, runs the risk of getting swept away by it. It is important that you stay calm and maintain your perspective on what is happening. But it can be hard to do that because toddler behavior often seems primitive and uncivilized. Well, guess what? It is! Civilization means a culture where people follow rules and laws, and toddlers don't always live in such a culture. They're just learning about rules and laws. Learning from you. It doesn't happen overnight. It takes time and patience.

As we've said, toddlers don't fight because they're "good" or "bad." Such labels deserve no place in your professional vocabulary. Toddlers fight because they know no other way to deal with their social problems. You wouldn't ask a toddler to balance a checkbook. Neither should you expect them to have the social skills to avoid conflict when it comes up. They're just not ready. Avoiding conflict is learned behavior. You as caregiver will be instrumental in teaching that behavior.

Before you go teaching children about conflict resolution, however, you'd better take a good hard look at yourself to see how good you are at it. Are you clear on the skills that are necessary to get you beyond interpersonal conflict? Among these skills are:

o   the ability to see the other person's point of view.

o   the empathy to understand how another person feels.

o   the willingness and ability to communicate clearly, and to let other people know what you need, feel, want, and think.

o   the sensitivity and self-awareness to predict how your behavior is going to impact on others.

o   the self-control to modulate your behavior if it seems disturbing to others.

o   the flexibility to think of different and alternate solutions to problems that may come up in your interactions with other people.

When you consider all the skills that an adult needs in order to navigate the social waters, you can begin to understand why it can be so hard for children to handle their social problems.

Remind yourself that toddlers are not developmentally ready to understand that others have a point of view. Their language skills don't allow for fast, easy communication. They have a poor grasp of cause and effect. Their emotions are often chaotic and overwhelming. With so few alternative strategies to fall back on, their immediate reaction to conflict is to respond physically. Push comes to shove, hit comes to bite, trouble breaks out.

A structured environment goes a long way toward preventing conflict. Three soft squishy balls offer a lot more opportunity to avert conflict than one ball will for the whole group.

Doling out play materials in the beginning of a session also helps, as toddlers have a very hard time sharing materials from a common pile. At this age, they'd rather hoard as much as they can.

Make a point of limiting the number of children playing in any one area. Too many children in one spot can be like too many rats in the maze: everyone gets frantic quickly!

Make sure toddlers have plenty of space. They may be small, but you would be surprised how much space a toddler can take up. In fact, toddlers take up more space than older children because they don't respect boundaries and as yet, don't have good control over their bodies. Watch and you'll see how they "accidentally" move into another child's space.

An ounce of distraction is worth a pound of cure. Redirect energies elsewhere as much as you can. If two children are in a dispute over a toy car, enlist one of them to help you water the plants.

When distraction and prevention just won't work and conflict does break out, the first order of business is to deal with the strong emotions that have become uncorked. Let the children know that you understand how they feel, but that first you must make sure everyone is safe and protected. Assure the children that you are there to help them solve the problem. Be assertive in removing the object in dispute—the toy car, the doll—so as to defuse the heated situation.

Once the children have calmed down, it's good to review the situation with them. That way, you can help them understand what happened and why. Always make a point of stressing cause and effect: "When Terry took your car, you got angry, Matthew, and you hit him." In other words, put everything out on the table for everyone to see.

Help the children solve the problem themselves. Talking about sharing is not going to carry any weight with children who have not yet reached the developmental plateau where they can understand what sharing is all about. Instead, demonstrate strategies that embody sharing in a way that they *can* understand. Help Terry find another car. Suggest that he might have just as much fun with the toy boat. Give him the kitchen timer, set for two minutes, and tell him that it will be his turn when the buzzer rings. Help him occupy himself while he's waiting for the two minutes to be up. Most important, make sure that your coping strategies take the needs of both children into account. Punishing one or both of the children is not constructive, and will not lead to problem-solving in the future.

Help the children by providing them with a "conflict vocabulary." If you're going to ask them to use their words, then they'll need those words, won't they? You might tell Matthew to say, "It's mine" when Terry is trying to pull the car from his hand. You might tell Terry to say "I want a turn" when

Matthew is hogging the treasured object. The words must be simple and must fall within the parameters of the children's language abilities. You can't teach a two-year old to say, "When you're finished with that, will you give it to me, please?"

Help children learn to find the help they need when they're having a problem. Make a distinction between "tattling" and asking for help.

Bugs and Germs, and Getting Sick

Prepare parents for the fact that when babies go into child care, they usually get sick more in the first few months than they would if they were at home. The good news, though, is that by the time child care kids go into kindergarten, they *never* get sick! They've got a set of antibodies that will protect them forever!

When adults begin to work in child care, they get sick as much as the children do. It takes a while for adults' antibodies to kick in, but once they do, they're in great shape.

The key to staying healthy when you work with kids is to wash your hands, wash your hands, wash your hands, and then wash your hands. You may begin to feel like an obsessive compulsive, but don't worry about it. It really makes a huge difference.

Lots of children are plagued by ear infections and very often, the first ones to notice the symptoms are the child care providers. The quicker you catch an ear infection, the easier it is to treat, so child care providers need to be alert to the symptoms: the baby doesn't seem to hear you; the baby starts talking louder; the baby is grumpy; or the baby is pulling on her ear.

Middle ear infections are the root of more than 90 percent of hearing problems in children under the age of six.

Make sure to let other parents know whenever a child in your care comes down with something contagious. Parents can pick up on symptoms more quickly when they know what they're looking for.

Sometimes, parents get very worried when their babies get sick. You can reassure them that children in group care build up great immunities and, in the long run, aren't any sicker than other kids.

Chapter 9

SHAKE, RATTLE, AND ROLL

hildhood is all about growth—intellectual, emotional, social, and physical—and that can be as challenging as it is exciting. Children are constantly growing and developing, and in the physical arena alone, need a good variety of toys and equipment to facilitate and promote both large- and small-motor development. Children also will look to their caregivers for new games and activities that will stimulate and support both kinds of growth.

While it is important to encourage motor development, whether it be of the gross- or fine-motor type, it is very important for child care providers to respect the fact that not all children develop at the same pace. Some children sit earlier, some later. Some children are early crawlers or early walkers, or can feed themselves early on, while others take their time crossing those thresholds. It's the job of a child care provider to respect these differences, to never rush a child who is developing at a slower pace, and to be alert and sensitive to the possibility of any developmental delays.

Identifying a possible developmental delay can be tricky, and child care providers need to walk a fine line between letting parents know when they should be concerned and not offering up any premature diagnoses that can alarm parents unnecessarily. Many slow starters develop into physically adept individuals. It just takes them a little longer.

Sometimes, the growth of young children almost can seem explosive and uncontainable. A child can come into the center in the morning and seem inches taller than he was the night before. Toddlers can have loud voices and make awkward, sudden moves. When my younger son was three, his nursery school teacher told us, very confidently, that he thought Nat had a hearing impairment because he spoke in such a loud voice. His teacher was a very, very quiet man who ran a very, very quiet classroom. My son was always bursting at the seams with barely containable enthusiasm for everything he did. We invited the teacher to dinner at our home where he met a family who all spoke in loud voices!

Many toddlers and preschoolers have a hard time knowing when to stop. As a caregiver, you sometimes may find yourself at wit's end, trying to cope with an energy level that far exceeds your own. If you're a quiet and sedentary sort of person, it may be very hard to be around that level of energy hour after hour. You may grow resentful; you may feel turned off by certain children; you might even call them "wild."

Don't.

That kind of label is unfair, inaccurate, and often it is arbitrarily used, designated along gender lines. In other words, a lot more boys are called "wild" than girls. Ask yourself, as a responsible caregiver, whether you are bringing any bias to this issue. Does part of you have a hard time tolerating a lot of noise and movement? Do you find yourself pulling kids out of physical play to give them "time out" with the idea that this will "calm" them?

Don't.

Or, at least, try not to. Even though some caregivers believe that it is beneficial to give active children this type of "time out," the fact is that removing a child from physical play who needs to move can create more problems than it solves. These children genuinely *need* to move. Confining them to chairs is a harsh punishment. It makes much more sense to get them outside where there is plenty of space, and encourage them to run. To be sure, some toddlers are placid and just like to stay put, but a great many others are naturally lively and energetic. These toddlers never should be labeled with words like "wild," "hyperactive," or "out of control."

Movement matters to toddlers; it contributes to their sense of well-being, particularly when they are in the 12- to 24-month period. By taking away opportunities for that movement, you may be creating an irritable, restless, and tantrum-prone child.

It is your role as a caregiver to provide the best and healthiest facility for your children. That means lots of movement and exercise, and you don't have to wait for the first warm sunny day to begin. Movement and exercise are not just outdoor activities. A child care facility has to allow for toddlers to move around freely indoors as well as out. In order for the children to practice their gross-motor movement, all interior spaces must be safely arranged.

Now let's listen as some caregivers share the tips they've gathered along the way.

One thing I make sure to have in our center is a soft indoor play area. You simply can't be without one. Every child needs a place where he can throw himself around as much as he likes and know that no harm will come to him. It's easy to create what I call a "soft safe spot." Get a bunch of pillows, mats, mattresses, moving pads, foam rubber blocks, or whatever else is available to you. The rest takes care of itself.

I've found that children adore obstacle courses. It's the hamster in them! So I've rigged up something in my room that they love. I found this enormous cardboard packing tube, as big around as three kids, and my two- and three-year olds just love to go burrowing through it. I hook it onto a platform made out of plywood boxes covered with carpet so no one can get splinters, with a couple of little ramps here and there. The children can spend hours on that thing, crawling and climbing, and stretching those growing muscles of theirs.

After years of watching kids, I have to say that there is a universal impulse, certainly among the boys, to build forts. I don't mean this to sound gender-biased: I would never limit what girls or boys do. It's just a reflection of experience. I guess it's that basic territorial instinct we all have. So I do what I have to do to accommodate that instinct. I line up chairs with blankets over them or use big bolster cushions pushed together to create a "fort-like" place. It doesn't matter to them how "fort-like" it is, just as long as some of them can defend it against the others. Remember the Alamo!

Dancing is a great way to get those gross-motor skills going. The kids love all kinds of dancing. Sometimes I'll put on "Hava Nagila." We'll clear a big space and what a workout we'll have! Or maybe we'll have "Dance Hour" when everything has to be done in time to the music. Did you ever see children bringing their dishes to the sink to the tune of the Macarena? It's a riot!

If you want to get children moving, there's nothing better than the old tried and true games. I'm thinking of ones like Duck, Duck, Goose, Goose and Red Light, Green Light. Those games are really magic and the teachers have just as much fun with them as the kids.

We play a game that everyone enjoys called "Parachutes." Here's how you do it. You take a sheet—also known as the parachute—and all the kids take hold of the edges and lift it way up high, then let it float down. Then I call out their names. When they hear their name, they try to run under the parachute and then run back out to home base before the parachute touches their heads. It's really a lot of fun. A variation on that is to place a ball or a balloon in the center of the parachute. Then you try to keep it in the middle or bounce it up and down without losing it. More fun!

Pushing and pulling is an important motor activity for children. I make a point of having on hand toy shopping carts, doll carriages, little toy lawnmowers they can use in the backyard, wagons, riding toys that they can sit on and propel with their feet, and the usual pull toys. These are among the most popular toys at the center.

I think there's a great benefit, in terms of motor development, of keeping a great big basket full of toys in the room and having the kids dump them out, carry them around, collect them, and put them back. It also sets them right up to do house-work in the future!

I believe that you have to present challenges to toddlers. In fact, I never met a toddler who didn't like to be challenged. But you have to make sure those challenges are safe and attainable. If you don't invite them to "push the envelope" a little, they are going to go looking for challenges in other places that may not be so safe.

When we think about exercise, most of us flash to the gross-motor skills: climbing, seesaw-ing, sliding. But let's not forget the importance of fine-motor skills and the need to exercise those, too. I make sure to involve the kids as much as I can in fine-motor practice. That means pouring their own milk at snack time, using a fork and a spoon, buttoning up their coats and zipping their pants, washing their hands, and learning to tie shoelaces. Sure, they need help getting started, but so what? That's what we're here for.

Little ones love to play freeze tag. They especially love it if they have to stop still in a very silly pose.

If you're working with young children, I think it's important to have good resources to help develop their fine-motor skills. I use a lot of art supplies in my room. I'm talking about finger paints, paint brushes, crayons, markers, and pencils. Then, beyond the art supplies, I always makes sure I'm well supplied with play-dough, blocks, push-button telephones, shape boxes, mini cash registers, beads for stringing, musical instruments, and so on.

Whenever possible, I try to keep the group size small. The best thing is if I can go out with just a couple of kids. We'll take a walk in the park, and look at the trees and flowers. The exercise is going on, but there's also some good learning happening, thanks to the small group.

I like to give children the chance to see adults modeling physical fitness as a way of life. A couple of the kids in our center have parents who are runners. Whenever they're in a race, even if it's on the weekend, I suggest we all go to the park to watch. Some do, some don't, of course. But the kids who do show up see adults who are fit, active, and serious about their health.

It's really fun for the children to encounter people in their neighborhood who are doing things with their hands. For instance, I might take different small groups of two or three out to the Italian grocery down the block from us, and we'll watch the man who owns it make fresh pasta. They love it! We used to have this old-fashioned shoemaker in the neighborhood and he would let the kids watch as he fixed the shoes. When you think about it, there are many people right under our noses who are demonstrating fine-motor skills such as the butcher, the baker, and the candlestick maker. The kids see them, and sometimes when we go back to the center, we'll role-play what we've just seen.

Some people are very uncomfortable with the idea of wrestling, but I find that some kids thrive from that kind of activity. Play-wrestling with preschoolers can be a great physical outlet as long as it's closely supervised by an adult and the rules ("Just yell 'no' when you want to stop) must be spelled out.

We put on an annual circus. Kids do imaginary tightrope walking, they hang on the swings set, they dress up like lions, and roll down hills. It's great fun and all the parents come to watch.

The best way to work off steam with toddlers and preschoolers is to jump. We have a jump-to-music time every day. We follow it with story time. It's a great sequence because by the time we sit down together to read, everyone is VERY ready to sit down!

Fantasy play is a great pathway to physical play. Ballerinas can spin, and super-heroes can fly, all in the scenario of make-believe play.

Balls of all sizes are a great spark for physical play. Kids especially love those enormous "exercise" balls that you can roll around on. You need to be careful, though, that little ones who are not steady on their feet don't lean on them and fall.

I've fought my impulse to always put a stop to roughhousing. Instead, I watch very closely to make sure it doesn't get out of hand. If it does, I step in and say, "Someone is going to get hurt if you do this. Let's try another game." If it goes well without my interference, I always compliment the children on how safely they played.

Sometimes, children who are a little slower physically get teased by kids who are more coordinated. It's something I talk to kids about privately. "It hurt Suzie's feelings when you teased her for being a slow runner." But more important, I always try to find each kid's area of strength. "Suzie might be the slowest runner but she's the fastest at solving puzzles." Rather than point out the contrast, I point out the strength where it's appropriate.

It's important to find a balance between physically active time and quiet time, and make sure each child gets a balance. We always have a physically active time just before lunch.

When we hit the local playgrounds, I try to stay in the background and let the kids shape their own activities. I only step in if there's a problem, or if they seem stuck and can't think of what to do, which hardly ever happens.

We get children outside to play in all kinds of weather. As long as there's not any lightening, they love to be in the rain. They jump in puddles and splash, and look for shelter between bushes. It's a pain to get everyone dressed and out in the winter, but it's well worth it. They come in all rosy-cheeked, and ready for lunch and nap.

Kids love to play with a hose or a sprinkler. They make up all sorts of games, but are usually happy to just run under or over the stream of water. Make sure that they're wearing plastic shoes, or if they're barefoot, do a sweep of the grass or sidewalk to make sure it's safe.

Sometimes when the play gets physical, boys and girls split up. It's fine to let kids take the lead with this, but you have to be careful that little girls who are agile and athletic get plenty of opportunity to express themselves, and to have their talents appreciated by everyone.

When kids get involved in physical play, they often set up teams, and they can be brutal with each other when they do it. "We don't want Gregg on our team. He stinks." If you see this happening, it helps to set the teams up for them, even if they complain. Also, if you've enforced Vivian Paley's rule—You Can't Say You Can't Play—it's a good time to remind everyone about it. You can even say, "You can do that when you're not in school, but here in school it's not allowed."

These days, by the time kids are four or five, they're often playing on actual competitive, organized teams. Most experts agree that this is too young to foster competition. Make sure that if your preschoolers play soccer or basketball, it remains low key and fun. Don't help them keep score!

Preschoolers love to play spinning games. The goal seems to be to spin until you're dizzy and fall down. It's very important that these games are played in a safe environment so no one goes careening into a wall.

When children become involved in physical play, it's important to teach them to respect differences. Some kids approach physical play by throwing themselves into things. Others like to stand and watch for a while before they play. Remind children that they shouldn't be pushy. Even a two-year old can learn to say, "People are different." Although they may not understand the full implications of what they are saying, over time they will learn, especially with the help of a teacher who values differences.

Kids also wind down differently. For some kids, the transition from wild and woolly outside roughhousing to quiet time is an easy one. Other kids need to slow down in stages. Don't expect the same from everyone. Give plenty of warning: "Five more minutes." Even if they don't know what "five minutes" means, they'll come to learn.

Chapter 10

THAT'S ENTERTAINMENT!

ave you ever watched children at the circus, at a puppet show, or at a children's theater performance? Their faces are utterly rapt as they sit there, enchanted by the spectacle before them. Most children have an intense desire to be entertained and a vast willingness to surrender to the make-believe.

Children also have an enormous capacity to entertain themselves. When my son Noah was three, Rachel, one of the girls in his child care, decided to be a doctor. She'd come to school each day with her stethoscope and open up her office. She was incredibly serious, responsible, and professional. Each day, Rachel's friends would sit on chairs that they'd set up in her waiting room and a receptionist would usher them in to the examining room, one by one.

Over the course of a week, the number of patients grew. Finally, by the end of the week, Rachel was at her wit's end. She walked out of her office, took a look at all of the people waiting to see her, and screamed, "It's too many patients. We need another doctor!" Fortunately, there was another doctor in the house.

That's how real the world of make-believe is to young children. And a good child care center should provide plenty of opportunity for it to flourish through music, story telling, amateur dramatics, and dress-up. This is the magic that turns an ordinary day into something special.

Music, Music, Music

The great German philosopher Friedrich Nietzsche once said, "Life without music would be a mistake." But we're sure you're not planning to make any such mistake in your room. Here are some thoughts from your fellow child care workers about how to make music an important part of the environment you create for children.

Model a love for music. If you don't see yourself as a music lover, ask yourself why that is. Were you criticized at some point in your life for being "tone-deaf" or "off key"? If you have bad associations to music, try to get beyond them for two reasons: one, you don't want to spread your negativity to the children, and two, you are missing out on one of life's foremost pleasures.

Get into your singing. You don't have to be good (although chances are you are fine). Remember Murphy Brown on her comedy series, how she'd have the time of her life belting out "You Make Me Feel Like a Natural Woman" full throttle? That should be you! If nothing else, you can be sure your children won't be harsh critics.

If you watch professional singers like Barbra Streisand, Sting, or Celine Dion, you'll see how they emphasize their singing with well-chosen hand and body movements. You should follow their lead and make up your own hand gestures and movements because the children will love this extra added ingredient. In the case of "The Itsy-Bitsy Spider," for instance, you can create a whole pantomime of movements with the spider climbing, the rain falling, and so on. If you do this, the children will soon learn to copy your movements, and even if they don't know all the words, they can use these movements as a way to feel involved.

Sing out and be proud, but once the children join in, you might want to start singing more softly.

That way, the children can hear themselves and each other, and they can become the leaders.

Don't make a fuss about the "right" words. Sure, James Taylor writes good lyrics, but he won't mind if the children don't follow the original that closely. They can have fun making up their own words or singing along in a free-spirited la-la-la way. And who knows? They might even come up with some winning rhymes.

Children delight in hearing or seeing themselves perform. Tape recorders are great for that purpose. Video cameras are even better. You can record the children singing, then play it back for them when they're dancing!

Play musical games. "Statue" or "freeze" are fun ones to play with lively contemporary music. A conga line snaking through the room can be a treat. Use your imagination!

Don't feel like you have to stick to kiddie songs when you play music or sing with young children. Billboard's top ten are great, as long as they are okay for kids under 13! Given how much toddlers love to sing, move, and dance, you'll want to provide them with a range of tempos, rhythms, and beats. That means you should play all kinds of music: rock, hip hop, Latin, country-western, jazz, show tunes, the whole nine yards.

When playing a wide range of music, preview it first for content. A lot of what is being recorded these days is shockingly inappropriate for young ears (and even older ones!).

Survey parents about their children's tastes in music. It's great to have a sense of what a particular child likes. Then, on a special day, like a birthday, you might surprise and delight the child by playing a favorite, whether it be "Abiyoyo," "Hey Jude," or "Peter and the Wolf."

When you're teaching a new song, always sing it through by yourself from start to finish so the children can hear the whole thing and appreciate the musicality of it. If you try to teach a song line by line, you run the risk of losing the children to boredom before they even get to the chorus.

Music can be a good way to draw out the feelings of children. When there is anger in the room, you can all let off steam by doing a war dance with whoops and hollers. If the mood in the room is sad for some reason, then maybe it's time for everyone to sing the blues together.

Music is wonderful, but, like all good things, there can be too much of a good thing. For many caregivers, background music is a nice way to create a feeling in the room, but some child developmental specialists feel that constant background music can become a distraction for babies who are trying to focus in on human voices. Some feel that a continuous musical soundtrack in the room can even inhibit the development of language which is a vital activity in the two- to three-year-old range. Therefore, many caregivers restrict music to particular purposes like movement time or lullabies at nap time. See what works best for you.

Be cautious about the volume at which you play music. If the music is too loud, it can not only jangle the sensitive nerves of babies but also even lead to hearing loss. Music should be played at moderate volume only. What's moderate? A volume at which the children can hear your voice while the music is playing.

Some children like to listen to music with a headset. Tape recorders that are designed especially for children have a preset limit on the volume control so that the music never plays loud enough to damage children's ears. If they are using a regular adult tape/CD player, you need to be very careful that the volume is low.

Music is a great way to learn about different cultures and languages. Make an effort to play songs from all over the world. There are many wonderful collections for children that offer international selections.

Kids can become very attentive to dynamics when they're singing. Teach them to sing softly, and to sing loudly, and to sing every way in between. Some songs—"Pop Goes the Weasel"—are designed with great big bursts in mind.

Some children's songs allow you to fill in the blanks with the names of the children in your group. Kids love customizing songs.

Don't be afraid to reach back in time to some old favorites like "You Are My Sunshine." There's a reason these songs are called "standards." They're very appealing to kids as well as to adults.

Kids love live performances. Check out your community for children's entertainers. Call local church groups and schools for suggestions. Plan a big musical event and invite kids and parents. It feels very special, and if the entertainers are good, they'll find a way to incorporate the kids into the program.

Making Musical Instruments

We can't think of a better rainy day activity than making homemade musical instruments. But then again, what a great activity for sunny days, too! Playing music on instruments that they make themselves is a thrilling experience for children and can greatly stimulate musical appreciation. At the same time, making and playing instruments offers little ones the advantage of developing their small-motor control.

As a caregiver, you'll want to remember to hoard all kinds of things that can be used for the above purposes. But don't forget to make a wish list and ask people for things as well. Stationary stores, supermarkets, bakeries, hardware stores: there is surplus everywhere just waiting to be turned into instruments!

Here are some tried and true "recipes" for instruments.

Drums

Start with a sturdy container. A round oatmeal box is excellent, a margarine tub, a coffee can, or a Crisco® can that is covered with a plastic snap-on lid. In fact, the end of any cylindrical container can be covered with scraps of fabric or maybe even leather, if you

have some hanging around. Different surfaces—
leather, cloth, paper—make different sounds that you
and the children can explore together.

Drumsticks

Kids can always use their hands for drumsticks. Or
you can use things like dowels, spoons, or chopsticks.
Keep in mind, though, that anything pointy should be
wrapped with cloth, cotton batting, or whatever will
protect little eyes. Different sound effects will be
heard depending on what material you use to wrap
the drumsticks. Also, make certain that no one runs
around holding a drumstick.

Shakers

What great rhythm-making you can get with shakers!
Almost anything will work: plastic film containers
(make certain to secure the lids with duct tape), plastic
eggs that once held Silly Putty, a baking powder can, a
little box that once held pins. Just look around. You
can achieve a variety of sounds depending on what
you insert into the container such as rice, dried beans,
different shapes of pasta (pastina makes a whole different sound than penne), coins, buttons, whatever.
Just make sure you tape the lid securely to the container (duct tape works well) so that no little objects
that might wind up in ears and noses can escape. You
also can use paper plates to make shakers. Simply staple two plates together after you've inserted the noise-
making substance inside (beans, macaroni, and the

like). Then staple all around the edges, keeping the staples very close so nothing can escape, and cover the edge with tape to make it smooth. Holes can be punched and string or rubber bands inserted so that the plates can be worn as "musical" birthday hats!

Rhythm Sticks

Same idea as drumsticks. Use dowels, bamboo fishing poles, or garden stakes. Cut them 12 to 15 inches long. Try painting them or applying shellac to create different tones. Chopsticks, spoons, or rungs from old chairs also can be used. If sticks are not covered with batting (and you may want to leave some uncovered so as to produce different sounds), supervise carefully to prevent any accidental (or intentional) poking.

Tambourines

The construction of a homemade tambourine is a little more complex than that of a drum or shaker, but you can do it. Here's how. Take the bottle caps from bottles of soda or water and remove the cork lining. Flatten the caps, making sure there are no sharp edges, and punch holes in them. Tie the caps to the edges of paper plates or, for even better effect, aluminum pie pans. Voila! A tambourine!

Swish or Sandpaper Blocks

Don't forget those scratchy-sounding blocks that kids love. They're a cinch to make. Just glue sandpaper to one side of a 2" x 2" x 1" wooden block with the rough side of the sandpaper up. You might recycle some old building blocks for this purpose. Just make sure that the blocks are smooth and without splinters. Then rub the sandpaper surfaces of two blocks together for a really satisfying sound.

Cymbals and Bells

Your little percussionists simply must have cymbals and bells, so here's how to make them. For cymbals, you can use jar lids, pot lids, or those indispensable aluminum pie plates again. A pot lid is great, of course, because it has its own handle, but for something that is handleless, you can glue on a wooden spool for a handle. (Make sure the spool is big enough so it won't present a choking hazard if it comes loose.) Then bang away!

Finger cymbals anyone? Just punch two holes in the center of two matching jar lids, two large buttons, or two bottles caps. Take a fat rubber band, fold it in half, and push each end through the holes. Insert thumb and forefinger through the loops and you've become a Romany (what we used to call "Gypsy" before we found out that term was culturally sensitive).

Another fun way to make bell sounds is by sewing small sleigh bells—which you can acquire for minimal money at a craft outlet—onto a wide piece of elastic. This gives you a wrist band of bells. Tra la la!

Kazoos and Horns

Tape waxed paper (or affix it with a rubber band) over one end of a cardboard tube, such as you're left

with when you finish a roll of paper towels or toilet
tissue. Then experiment by making sounds into the
open end. You'll get different sounds if you punch
holes in the tube. Alternatively, you can use empty
soda bottles of different sizes for horns. Blow across
the mouth of the bottles and you'll see how different sizes produce different tones. This can be difficult for young children to do, so stay closely tuned
for any building frustration.

Banjos and Guitars

You'll be paddlin' Madeline home when you make
your own little banjos and gee-tars. Start with a shoe
box (have you gotten the idea yet that a smart caregiver *never* throws anything away?). Then cut a large
hole in the middle of the lid, and cut a piece out of
the end of the lid and the end of the box. Take one
of those cardboard tubes (the ones from the paper
towels or toilet tissue that you *never* throw away)
and cut a slit in it. Insert the tube into the opening
you've made in the shoe box. Stretch nice sturdy
rubber bands across the box, spaced far enough apart
so that you can get your fingers in between them.
Slide a pencil or a short piece of cardboard tube
under them. "Tune" the banjo using different size
rubber bands. Then pluck away!

Water Chimes

We've never met a child who wasn't enchanted by
this way of making music. Take eight glasses. Start

on one end with the glass practically full and, going down the line, put less water in each of the next seven glasses so by the time you reach the last glass, there is very little water in it. Then see how the tone of the full glass sounds compared to the one next to it and the one next to that. By adding or subtracting water from each glass, you can make adjustments until you have the eight musical notes of a scale. Tap the glasses lightly with a spoon, a chopstick, your fingernail, a pencil, or whatever. If you want the notes to be short, place your finger on the rim of the glass. This works best with glass, not plastic, so close supervision will be necessary. But young children are very respectful of instruments once you explain that they are deserving of respect.

Dance

Martha Graham, the American genius who almost single-handedly created modern dance, once described dance as "the hidden language of the soul." It is a soulful spectacle to see people dance, particularly little people, who, when given the opportunity, throw themselves into movement with delightful abandon. Consider the following tips when you're thinking about your center and the role that dance can play in it.

Just as you modeled a love of singing, you should model a love of dancing. Don't be self-conscious about your dancing. Whatever you do, the children will love it, and if you give yourself half a chance, so will you!

When you work with young children, you become aware of how much energy they carry in their bodies and how important it is for them to have a positive outlet for that energy. Without a positive outlet, that energy can get translated into fidgety, squirmy, nonpositive behavior. Put on a record or play a simple rhythm on one of the homemade instruments above, and see how that nonpositive behavior can be channeled into the exhilarating movement we call dance.

Make room for dance; not only in the time of the day but also in the space you provide. Without enough space, there can be unfortunate collisions into other people and objects.

Start simply. Don't think of yourself as a grand ballet master. All you want is for the dance movements to be fun and good exercise. Rule out any ideas of "right" or "wrong" when it comes to dancing. Empower the children. Let them think up new steps and movements. Playing a "copying" game, where one child initiates a movement and everyone copies her, can be fun for all.

Dancing can begin with simple warm-up exercises such as touching toes, stretching, jumping jacks, twisting at the waist, bending at the knees, bouncing, and hopping, all in time to the music. This is dance if you define dance as a heightened awareness of what your body can do when you can control it. A dance can be a parade and a parade can be a dance. Start clapping hands, and soon a line of children can be snake-dancing all through the child care center.

Another good way to initiate dance is by creating a movement game. Imitating movements is a fun game. All the dancers can take turns thinking of an animal and then trying to imitate its movement: a bunny's hop, a horse's gallop, a chicken's waddle, a worm's wriggle. Get the idea?

A variation on the above is what we call "pantomime dancing." In addition to the animal movements, a child could pretend to be a dancing ball or someone carrying a heavy suitcase. Or you could shudder like you're cold or sway like you're a willow tree in a windstorm. It's a fun game, but in order to keep it fun, remember not to turn it into a competition. Everyone is a winner just for joining in.

Try this. You're the "caller." You call out different parts of the body and the children have to move only that part. Swing arms, you call out, and there's a whole sea of swinging arms in front of you. Just one arm! Elbow dancing! (make circles with your elbows).

Musical games like Loopy Lou and the Hokey Pokey are perennial favorites for good reason: they're lots of fun.

Mix things up. Make sudden changes in the rhythm and tempo of the piece while the children dance. The idea is to get them attuned to musical elements like rhythm and tempo.

Props can add a whole other dimension to dance. Think of Fred Astaire. In one of his movies, his dancing partner was a coat rack! You could use towels, scarves, hats, or balls, whatever works.

After a while, you can make the dancing more challenging. Switch from calling out instructions— "jump, jump"—to jumping and see if the children follow you. Make one of the children the leader and see what happens. In simple, clear, but nonthreatening ways, you're upping the ante to see how it impacts on dance. If the impact is good, go with it. If it seems to be making the children nervous, scale back.

As children get older, they'll enjoy learning more structured forms of dance. Folk dances like the hora, the jig, and the Mexican hat dance are always fun. So are simple rounds and square dances. Older children can handle the need to be in time with the music and usually have the ability to carry out more complex instructions. Chances are, they'll enjoy the challenge.

Dancing can be very exciting and, as we know, it can be hard to wind down from something exciting. You can help the children wind down by playing the accompanying music softer and softer. Or perhaps, using the animal game again, you can go from the lusty hops of a kangaroo to the comic waddle of a duck to the slow, soothing steps of a snail. Or how about pantomiming a spaceship blasting off and then winding down to a floating feather descending to earth?

Dramatic Play

Children are natural hams. They love the spotlight and they love the chance to explore their fantasies by inhabiting other characters in imaginary situations. Set up a dramatic play stage at your center and you will discover what an effective tool it can be.

Create a "stage" in your room. Even a special rug will serve as a useful focus. If you want to be more ambitious, you might get a handy parent to help you build a platform.

Create and maintain a dramatic play area for the children. Keep dress-up clothes (usually items passed down by adults or picked up for pennies at thrift shops), a range of "uniforms" (chef's apron, sailor's slicker, and the like), and an assortment of props, from umbrellas to stuffed animals, dolls, and whatever else you think might come in handy. The old cereal boxes, empty juice and milk cartons, margarine bowls, and egg crates that you don't use for musical instruments described above are great for the play kitchen where a child can have fun imitating mom or dad.

NOTE: Different kinds of hats can be amusing but they can also spread head lice. It's better if the hats are plastic and the caregiver can wipe them down regularly.

Put on a show as often as the mood strikes. It can be set off by something that someone brings in from home. We once saw a wonderful little play, totally improvised, that was inspired by a yo-yo that one of the children "borrowed" from an older sibling.

Be aware that making a place for dramatic play in your room opens the door for all kinds of beneficial role-playing that you can utilize throughout the day. This role-playing can help teach cooperation, sensitivity, completing tasks, or any other subject that you feel must be addressed. And it's a wonderful way to resolve conflict as well.

Remember that the scripts for dramatic play should come from the children. That's the whole point. Don't expect them to act out your fantasies.

Dramatic play is invaluable for reinforcing such concepts as holiday observances, multiculturalism, community helpers, and so forth. It also can be used very discreetly to explore such sensitive issues as dealing with strangers, keeping your body private, and so forth.

Make room for applause and acclaim as part of the dramatic play in your center. Hearing applause and acclaim can do a great deal for a child's self-esteem, and it is appropriate in this context. In fact, dramatic play in general can go a long way toward making a shy, inhibited child into a more comfortable, outgoing one.

Recognize that dramatic play happens all the time when children work cooperatively. Kids who are building something with blocks are really setting a stage. Two children in the housekeeping corner who are making dinner are putting on a play. Rachel, the doctor we talked about at the beginning of this chapter, was completely involved in dramatic play, as were all her patients.

You can best support the dramatic play of young children in very subtle ways. Visit the doctor with a headache. Ask for a cup of tea. See if you can climb on the bus. Kids are very welcoming to adults who are willing to step outside of reality with them.

Chapter 11

PEOPLE WHO NEED PEOPLE

Working as a caregiver means working with people. If you don't like working with people, child care is not the career for you. Become a surveyor or a forest ranger or a diamond cutter. As a person who cares for very young children, though, you are constantly thrown together with all kinds of people: staff, parents, grandparents, and, of course, children. There's no doubt about it: to be successful in child care, you have to develop strong, positive resources for dealing with people.

Basic People Skills

Child care providers are enormously prone to burnout. One of the reasons for the burnout is that you are in a very high stakes profession (what could be more high stakes than being entrusted with the care and well-being of another person's child?), in which demands are constantly being placed on you ("I want a cookie," "I want my mommy," "Mickey said I was stupid," and so on). Couple that with the fact that you are probably not making very much money and not receiving very good benefits. In a child care setting, with all the demands being made, the opportunity for interpersonal friction is particularly high. Here are some ways that other child care providers have maximized their people skills.

I've made myself become a good listener. I wasn't always. In my family of origin, to make yourself heard, you had to shout. One day I just stopped shouting and decided to listen to the people around me. It has made a big difference. I don't think about what I'm going to say while they're talking, but, instead, I hear them and then frame a response. That's called give-and-take. That's called a conversation.

Children listen better when they are listened to. It's not something that can be taught, but it *is* something that can be learned if it's modeled by teachers.

Ask good questions. Being passive is never an interesting position to be in. When you're talking to someone whether a parent, another staff member, or even a child, solicit information from them. You'd be amazed how much people enjoy sharing things about themselves.

A very wise person once taught me a skill called mirroring. This is when you study and reflect another person's communication style. If the person is demonstrative and gestures with her hands, then you be demonstrative and gesture with your hands. If the person is reserved and speaks few words, you do the same. You have to keep it subtle; you don't want the other person to think you're imitating them. But when you mirror someone successfully, the other person feels that you're in harmony and it can lead to really effective interaction.

A huge source of stress in the field has to do with giving and receiving feedback. When you're a caregiver, you're in a performance situation. People will judge you; you will judge people. To successfully give feedback, I find that you have to be nonjudgmental. You have to be sensitive to the other person's resistance. And you have to limit your criticism to a specific action or behavior. Never make it into an indictment of someone's personality.

Give feedback only on things that the other person can change. If something can't be changed, don't bring it up. It's one thing to criticize someone because they don't pitch in and help; it's another to criticize them because they're bald. What's the point?

We teach children a lot about conflict resolution but how good are the adults at it? I'm working at it myself. One thing I've learned is never to say or do anything immediately. You know the old gimmick of counting to ten? It works. It gives you ten seconds of cool off time, usually enough to let some rational thinking flow back in.

When you get angry, it's really important to figure out what it is that's making you so angry. A lot of the time, the anger comes from buttons that are being pushed. For instance, you might go into a deep funk when your director asks you to work on your organizational skills. This could be a pretty straightforward suggestion, but you're in a rage because he's pushing buttons that go all the way back to your childhood, if, let's say, you had a parent who always belittled you.

If I get angry, I go for a long walk. The angrier I am, the longer the walk. Sometimes, I wind up all the way downtown before I even realize it!

Some people go on a drunken binge, some people wreck cars, but deep breathing is what I do when I get angry.

Ending conflicts can be complicated. Some people are wed to the idea of an apology. Don't be. There are times when you're never going to get an apology, and if that's all you'll settle for, the thing will never end.

It's very easy for child care providers to get into a thing where they're judgmental about parents. "If they didn't hold her all the time, she'd be more willing to crawl" or "If they didn't bring her into their bed, she'd have an easier time going down for a nap." That kind of attitude creates all kinds of problems. Child care providers really need to team up with parents. It's part of the job. It isn't always easy, but part of the job is finding ways to do it, like making pot-luck dinners, having parent meetings, or always making a point of telling parents special things about their babies.

If you need to confront someone who works with you (or for you), stick with the facts and deal with the present. Don't bring up a whole history of transgressions. "And then there was the time you did that and then there was the time you did that." Forget all that. It'll lead to nothing good.

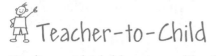

Teacher-to-Child

Dealing with children is not like dealing with adults. It's a whole other ball game and you have to know the rules. Even more, you have to develop an intuitive sense of what is right and natural around children. They seem to have a built-in phoniness detector, and a low tolerance for anything that is arbitrary and unfair. Once you speak their language, however, you'll discover what a wonderful language it is!

My cardinal rule as a caregiver is to make eye contact with children. I do this whether I'm praising them or disciplining them. Either way, I look them in the eye. Of course, that eye isn't always looking back at you. Sometimes I'll have to take a toddler's head gently in my hands and focus his face on mine while I'm talking. And I always reinforce the action by explaining what I'm doing: "I like you to look at me when I'm talking, Billy. That's why I'm holding your head." Whenever I interview a potential new staff member, I have them spend time in the room to see if they make eye contact with the children. If they don't, I pass on them.

I think you can tell a good caregiver by the way that he or she gets down to the child's eye level.

Put yourself in the child's place. Would you want this giant towering over you, telling you what to do? Of course not! So you bend down and establish some rapport. Sure, it's hard on the knees, but it's worth it.

When my favorite employee came in for an interview, I asked her to do a circle time with the three-year olds. She gathered everyone in a circle and said, "Hi. I'm Peggy, and I'm really hoping I get to work here with you guys." The way she talked to the children was the most natural thing in the world. She's been here ever since. The other day, I overheard her at circle time and remembered how much I loved her. She sat down, looked at all the kids and said, "So, I just got my hair cut. What do you think?" The kids love talking to her because they know that she really cares about what they say.

When I train staff, I always try to explain to them that one of the most important aspects of our job as caregivers is to promote language development. Some people we hire are very good, hard-working, and loving, but they may not realize that they have to talk to the kids. I tell them that language is the tool we use to build warm relationships with our children. When we talk to them, sing with them, joke with them, laugh and act silly with them—and I'm talking about even the tiniest infants—they come to know us as people and can respond to our verbal and nonverbal cues.

My approach to children is simple. I always think about what it means to be a responsible caregiver. These children need care, and I'm the one who can give it to them. If that means a blanket, a pacifier, or a snack, it's up to me to figure it out. And I like knowing that these tiny little human beings are thriving under my care. I know it's not the kind of work everyone dreams of, but it's the kind of work I've always dreamed of!

Listening to toddlers—and I mean *really* listening—can be hard. It takes a lot of concentration. Their speech can be slow and hard to understand. Make sure you're really patient and tolerant. When I was in grade school, I had a bit of a stammer, and I once had a teacher who imitated me. Can you imagine? She was my worst nightmare. When I started my career in child care, I did so with the pledge that I would never, ever, be any child's worst nightmare. So what if it takes them a while to form their words? I encourage my kids to speak and I try never to speak for them.

Talk with your toddlers. One of the most important things you can do with them is to be an active language partner. And you know what? A lot of toddlers I know are a whole lot more interesting than a lot of the adults I know. Really!

Pay special attention to toddlers who are shy, quiet, or withdrawn. Sometimes, you may wind up having one-sided conversations, but that's okay. This can actually go on for quite a while with some kids, but pretend otherwise. Make believe, even in a one-sided conversation, that your partner is keeping up his end of the deal. Just keep up the conversational flow (you can do a blow-by-blow description of what he's doing, for instance), and in time, the modeling may sink in and he'll start talking back.

Let yourself fall in love with a child if that's where your heart is going. Don't worry about favoritism. Loving one child in a special way doesn't mean you don't care for others. It's just that kids are people; sometimes the chemistry is better, and sometimes it's worse.

I make a point of repeating, expanding on, or restating what the child says to me. "Oh, so you like red? I like red too. Tomatoes are red. Fire engines are red." This way, the child knows that you've been listening and that you can understand what she is saying.

Don't plan for an infant to learn to talk and don't set any arbitrary deadlines in that regard. The sound of your voice and your everyday interactions are more than enough to create an environment in which the infant will begin to understand the connection between sounds and words.

Instead of labeling children as "problems," I try to figure out what the problem is. Usually, there's a pattern to behavioral problems, so I try to really examine the whole setting in which these problems are triggered. Maybe it's a particular activity that is overstimulating to a certain child. Maybe it's a very loud noise level that some kids just can't handle. Usually there's a reason, and if I modify the situation, the problem disappears.

As much as I can, I try to couch what I say from my perspective. That is, I don't say *you* as much as I say *I*. For example, I don't say "You're bad" when a child bites. Instead, I say, "I do not allow children to bite each other here." Or I'll have the biter look at the child he bit and say, "It hurts Johnny when you bite. See how he's crying?" I also try to break down the passivity of the kid who gets bitten by encouraging him to say, "You hurt me." Then, as fast as I can, I'll grab something appropriate to bite like an apple, and I'll hand it to him and say, "Apples/teethers/teddies are for biting," encouraging him to take a big bite from something that won't get hurt.

If a child is bitten by another child, it's important to wash the wound immediately with soap and water. If the bite breaks the skin, the child should be taken to her physician for a follow up. The wound should be covered with a sterile gauze bandage. If heavy bleeding is caused by the wound, emergency assistance must be called.

I make a point of looking for children's successes. For instance, I'll always try to catch kids being kind and loving to each other. The other day, one of our little boys fell off some climbing apparatus and he was crying. Another little boy went over to offer some comfort and I was quick to make a big deal about it. "What a good friend you are, Sam," I told him. "You saw that Antoine got hurt and you want to help him." Positive reinforcement works so much better than negative responses.

I think it's important for the children to really know who I am as a person. The more they know about me, the more they see me as a fellow human being. I tell them what it was like to grow up in Venezuela, to be the third of six children, to be the granddaughter of a fisherman, and that sort of thing. I even bring in pictures from my childhood. They love it!

It's very important for me to get to know the kids' families and have a sense of what their home is like. In a small center, you can always pay them a visit at home at some point in the first month that you're caring for them. Sometimes their parents make dinner which is really great! In a larger center, you can make it a point to connect with parents and siblings whenever they come by for pick-up or drop-off. Make the most of these times to get a sense of who the family is and to give them a sense of who you are.

I find reading a very important way to develop relationships with children. It is really a unique, quiet, intimate time. It also reinforces values that are the backbone of good relationships.

Don't create a screen around you with background noise. I've been to some centers where they keep the radio going all day. I even went to one where they had the television going. It was horrible! Make enough quiet space so the children can get next to you and have a conversation. At the same time, don't get hung up on having things be "oh so quiet" for infants. They'll do just fine with the low hum of everyday sounds in the room.

Take a break with a child. If you're tired and a child is tired, it's a nice time to scoop her up onto your lap. Maybe you'll want to read a book or magazine out loud. She might not understand the words or the pictures, but your voice, your words, and what you are doing will have an effect on her developing brain. Or maybe you want to skip the book, skip the magazine, and just "veg out." That's nice too!

Try to find a way to do something special, from time to time, with one child. That might involve a special story or song, or just some quiet time one on one.

I try my best always to be sensitive to gender discrimination and bias. That means I encourage gross-motor skills in both sexes. Girls can climb and run and jump just like boys, and boys can dance up a storm when given the opportunity. The same goes for doll-play, dress-up, painting, buttoning, puzzles, and drawing. None of these are for boys or girls, but for everyone. I also encourage the kids to create emotional dramas in their play with dolls, cars, trucks, and action figures. I let them know that they can be anything they want to be.

I give lots of wall space at the center to posters, pictures, and whatever I can get my hands on that shows the flexibility and breadth of gender roles.

I have a great poster up right now that shows a woman truck driver with the line "Mommy's Coming Home." The kids love it!

I encourage parents to come in who can demonstrate that occupations are open to both genders. I have a mom who is a cabinetmaker, a dad who is a nurse, and that sort of thing.

Whenever possible, I try to hire male care providers. They bring another dimension to the center. They model the fact that men can be nurturing and caring, and they're great at lifting heavy things!

Teacher-to-Parent

The relationship of caregiver to parent can be wonderfully supportive, a real partnership, or it can be fraught with tension. Here are some thoughts about how to make it work.

Create a parenting library in the room. Beg, borrow, and steal as many excellent books as you can about child development and parenting. Put "library cards" on them and sign them out. Establish yourself as a resource for constructive thinking about parenting.

Have lots of parenting magazines on hand and read them. If a parent is having a problem, you might be able to refer him to a useful article.

If you can, enlist some parents to help with a monthly newsletter from the center. You can desktop publish it on someone's personal computer, and fill it with stories about what's happening at the center, cute little features about the kids, recipes for fun snacks, and so on. It's a nice way to create community.

Parents need to know about what their children have been up to during the day. It's not enough for you to say, "Oh, it was fine," when mom or dad comes to pick up the kids. I keep an individual notebook on each child, and I write down any achievements, milestones, concerns, and whatever seems noteworthy. Some centers post these kinds of notes on a bulletin board. I think this is fine, too, although I know of cases where the parents have been made uncomfortable because then everyone knows what is going on with their child. Of course, I would get around that by not posting anything that I thought deserved confidentiality. I would not post, for instance, the fact that Terry bit another child that day. The whole world does not need to know that.

Schedule regular conferences with parents where you can talk in depth about how their child interacts with other children and staff. This kind of time is valuable for parents and caregivers alike.

 Schedule a few pot-luck dinners a year for parents and staff to get together for a social evening.

 As far as I'm concerned, television is a very destructive force in the lives of our children. It makes it much harder for them to concentrate and focus. I encourage my parents to limit the amount of television and video watching their kids are involved in. I also suggest that if television is a big presence in their home, parents should spend time watching it alongside the children.

 I try to get around the television problem by suggesting neat ideas for at-home activities to my parents. Making pretzels, playing music, or exercising: anything's better than the boob tube.

 A lot of parents at the center ask me for ideas for things their kids can do while they're busy making dinner or whatever. I suggest things like a special box of toys, simple puzzles, blocks, or story tapes.

I always call parents at work when something exciting happens. It doesn't matter how big their job. One of my mothers is a senior vice president of marketing at a Fortune 500 company. I got her in a meeting to tell her that her daughter, Cleo, took her first steps. Let me tell you, she didn't mind a bit!

If parents have a work e-mail, it's a great way to be in touch. Send them a note while their child is napping, just to update them on the day. They really appreciate it.

Appreciate the fact that parents are often under pressure from their own parents. And moms and dads don't always agree on things. There are all sorts of things going on in the lives of the families you care for, and you can take one load off their minds by being appreciative of the ways in which their child is special.

Although it isn't always feasible, whenever possible I encourage teachers to visit the home of incoming children because if you know what to look for, it's a great way to learn about the child. You can tell so much from a home environment. Are the parents formal? Is it an "anything goes" atmosphere? What's the sibling situation? Are there grandparents living there? It all goes into the big picture you form for each child.

I see part of my function as a caregiver to troubleshoot certain parenting problems. For instance, I had a mother who was very obsessive about her child's eating habits. She was frantic if he ate too much or too little. I gave her a couple of articles about children's eating habits and it settled her down.

An important tradition at our center is to periodically hold parents groups. All the parents get together and share information and insights about feeding, sleeping, naps, and discipline. It's a great way to learn, but more, it's a great way to build community. And community is what the center is all about. For many people living in our nation today, where so much is anonymous, it's the most vital kind of community they have.

Find something nice to say about each child to her parents. It really isn't all that difficult. The kids all have something special about them. Even if you only say, "Maria was in the most delicious mood today; she was all smiles," it's enough to make a parent feel great.

Be sympathetic to the stress so many parents are under, and the guilt many of them feel about not being with their kids full time. It's difficult to leave your baby with another person all day.

Chapter 12

CREATING YOUR OWN ENVIRONMENT

s a caregiver, you probably have spent a great deal of time watching children hard at work in your block corner. You've seen the marvelous structures they can create, sometimes even bigger than themselves. And you've seen the importance of creating a solid foundation for these structures. Without that foundation in place, the structure is shaky and in danger of collapse. Chances are you watched as the children learned for themselves the importance of a solid foundation.

Experienced child care providers know that the success of a child care center also depends on a strong foundation and solid structure. Great environments for kids don't just happen accidentally. They are the result of a great deal of thought and planning. Larger chains of child care centers benefit from resources they have available and the plans of architects who specialize in planning environments for young children. However, smaller child care centers can be very creative on a shoestring budget.

The Philosophy

Most centers are built on some kind of philosophy of how to care for young children. Some centers stress learning, perhaps more than they should. There is a huge amount of pressure today to make every moment of a child's life academic, starting in the crib. Earlier in this book, we discussed what gets lost amid this kind of pressure; that is, the recognition that for infants, *every* moment is a learning moment. ABCs, number facts, and any other kind of background "academic" stimulation isn't necessary. Natural life experiences are the best kind of learning experiences at this age.

The most compelling reason to allow your babies just to be babies is that they'll never have that opportunity again. Too much child care today is about getting kids "ready" for the next stage of their lives rather than letting children enjoy the stage that they're in. Most of the child care providers we spoke with felt very strongly about that issue.

They also felt that the very best child care centers were the ones that tried to imitate the home environment as closely as they could. When it works, the home environment is still the best model we have for child care. In this chapter, providers like yourself talk about some of the ideas that underlie their centers, the ideas that have given them the form and strength that was needed.

It's all about flexibility. We have to remember that we're dealing with very young children here. They can't punch a clock. They can't be worried about a lot of rules. Some rules are great and I wouldn't be without them—not throwing blocks comes immediately to mind or not walking around with a bottle— but too many rules can lead to an institutional feeling that never feels right to the kids. Take eating, for instance. Infants need to eat when they're hungry, not on a schedule.

I love it when a child shows up for the day in her pajamas. It means to me that the center is like home to her, and that's what a center should be. And it also means to me that the parents are relaxed enough with the routine that they aren't going to worry about breaking the "rules." You know, one of these days I may even show up in my pajamas!

I've visited centers where the schedule is so "arranged" that it seems there is more attention given to the time of day than to the needs of the children. In my center, if story time goes on a half-hour longer, that's fine with me. We have no bells that ring here. When these kids get to high school, they can start listening for bells. They've got the rest of their lives to listen for bells. Here, we go with the flow.

The Set Up

When we first arrived at Basic Trust with Noah so many years ago, it was on the bottom floor of a brownstone in New York City. The good news is that there was a backyard, right in the middle of the city. The bad news is the space was very small and it had terrible light. Somehow, though, it didn't seem to matter. The emotional environment at Basic Trust was so remarkably warm and filled with light that no one felt deprived. We didn't really have a sense of how "bad" our space was until we moved to a new space that was fabulous. It was a series of rooms in an old public school, huge rooms that were flooded with light from enormous windows. There was plenty of space in the toddler room for a big, custom-built climbing gym. And the babies had their own sleep room that was carpeted and dark, and quiet.

I guess the point is that it's great to have a great space. And it's important to think about how you design your space when you're setting up a center. Kids need a safe environment with lots of light. It's ideal if you can manage to have some access to the outside. Nothing, however, is more important than filling whatever space you create with love. If you think that sounds corny, you're probably not in the right business. Child care providers are never afraid of sounding corny!

Don't be blinded by glitzy equipment, but don't underestimate the value of a well-designed, safe space. The most important thing, of course, is for teachers to be warmly interactive with kids, but a center that has wonderful blocks, climbing equipment, bright space, a cozy nap room, and great art/music/dress-up certainly has a leg up.

At our center, we purchased used preschool chairs, used book shelves, used cubbies, a used art easel, used doll houses, and anything else used we could get our hands on.

Whenever you buy used equipment, it's important to make sure it meets all current safety standards, isn't damaged in a way that could pose a danger to kids, and that it hasn't been recalled.

It helps to be creative. I do a lot of scavenging on the street. You wouldn't believe what I've found: lamps, screens, fans, books, rugs, all free and better than what I'd go out and buy!

The money I save can go for things I can't find on the streets like manipulatives or musical instruments. And just a step up from free on the streets are thrift shops, tag sales, and salvage companies. Keep looking!

I like to think of my room as my partner. By this I mean that the room can teach just as much as I can. I reinforce as many concepts as I can through the room decor with colors, shapes, and cultural diversity. It's all displayed all over my room.

Make a point of labeling. My staff calls me The Label Queen. I go around with my magic marker and my sticky tabs putting names on things all over the place: piano, window, sink, trash. It's that subliminal message that works better than sitting children down and "teaching" them their ABCs before they should be worrying about such things. For children who aren't reading yet, it's always great to include a picture with your label.

Young children are working at the job of organizing the world around them. There's so much to keep track of. One way I help them is by organizing the center. I think it's very important to create different "mini centers" within the center at large. This reinforces the children's classification and organization skills. Therefore, I have a snack center, a "library," an art center, and so on. That way everyone knows where everything is.

I encourage all child care providers to take a good hard look at their rooms and ask themselves if they see enough interesting things. Do your walls look barren? Or is there too much to look at? Is it hard to focus in on any one thing? The thing to aim for is a harmonious balance, energy, and space at the same time.

The kids' art should go right up on the walls or the cork board. And artwork should be hung at a height where the kids can see it. That means that in the baby room where you've got lots of crawlers, the artwork should be way down low. You can also hang a few at parents' level, just to avoid lower back pain!

It is important to arrange your room so that you can see all the spaces easily. Don't create divisions in the room with bookcases; that makes for hidden places you can't monitor. You want to be able to interact with the children and do a quick 360-degree bird's eye view of the room every few minutes, heading off problems at the pass before they have time to develop.

Interaction with Infants

Consider the quality of your interaction with children. Is it everything you want it to be? The needs of infants are particularly specific. The right kinds of interaction are an invaluable preventative against troublesome behavior. Toddlers need lots of space, but an infant room can be small with everything in easy reach.

Whenever you deal with infants, make sure that they can see your face. They want to watch you and learn from your expressions. Use a lot of eye contact and smile freely. You'll be repaid with lots of delicious infant smiles!

Don't make yourself crazy trying to provide infants with an endless amount of visual stimulation. There are plenty of interesting things for infants to look at in the "natural" environment around them. Infants are interested in things that we regard as so ordinary that they escape our attention. An infant, lying on her back, can be just as fascinated with a lighting fixture, for instance, as by a fancy mobile. If you do want to construct something special, there's no need to run out and spend a lot of money. You can tie a wooden spoon or some measuring spoons to the crib with a short elastic, making sure that it's safe and secure, and the infant will focus in on that. Eventually, in about six months, she'll be batting at it and having the time of her life!

Never have anything "hanging" in a crib once a baby is able to sit up. It poses a choking hazard.

I like to change the visual environment for my infants from time to time, so I use the kind of hook that stays in the ceiling and I hang different mobiles at different times.

When an infant gets bored, he turns away from what he's looking at. Child development experts call that "habituation." When I notice that my infants aren't looking at things around them, then I know it's time to change the surroundings.

I always make a point of carefully watching what an infant is looking at. Some infants are drawn to color, some to motion, some to people's faces. Then I try to provide different things for different infants, depending on their "personal preferences."

I'm always careful not to overdo it when I get new infant toys; otherwise, it becomes too overwhelming. One new toy at a time is best, so the infant has time to explore it before you move on to the next. I'm talking about a few days or even longer between introductions.

Diapering is not just about maintenance. It's a really great opportunity for a caregiver to connect to an infant and make eye contact. Whenever I diaper an infant, we bond a little just through our eyes.

Keep a bottle of diluted bleach solution in a mister and always spray down the table after each diaper change so that it's clean for the next one.

There are several advantages to keeping your changing table up against a wall. For one thing, it's safe and secure. Also, we usually put up some great pictures on the wall: close-up shots of faces are ideal. Sometimes, I put a shiny piece of mylar on the wall because infants love the reflections and all the light. Depending on baby/teacher ratios, it's a good idea to set up the changing table so you can look out at the room while you're diapering.

Cut out lots of great pictures of faces from magazines and laminate them on both sides. You can either buy a good laminator—which you'll have lots of use for—or buy clear contact paper. Then get these little Velcro buttons or squares and attach them to the back of the cutouts. You won't have any problem changing the decor of the changing table any time you want to.

I like to keep toys at the changing table so babies can hold them while they're being changed. Little stuffed animals or rubber squeeze toys are just right.

Think of diapering as an occasion for real one-on-one interaction. You should be talking to the baby about what you're doing or what they're doing while the changing is going on. That's the kind of "learning" that makes sense, not standing there with flashcards.

The changing area should be really well thought out. Everything should be in arm's reach. The better the design, the less chance there is of an accident, the quicker the work gets done, and the more time is left over for things that are fun to do.

Diaper Duty Do's and Don'ts

Always have everything you need for a diaper change within easy reach of the changing table.

Never take both hands off a baby while you are changing a diaper. They can move much faster than you think!

Have a dispenser with plastic bags and twisties handy so that you can seal up dirty clothing and dirty diapers. You can cut a hole in a bleach bottle and fill it with the plastic bags you get at the supermarket. Just pull one out when you need it.

Put the soiled diapers in a container with a tight fitting lid. You don't want toddlers to explore the dirty diaper bin.

Always wipe from front to back. When you're finished wiping the baby, use a clean wipe for your own hands.

When you're all done, make sure to wash your hands and the baby's hands. It's an important way to keep infections from spreading.

When you're finished and the baby is back on the floor, spray the changing table with a bleach solution. To make bleach solution, mix 1 tablespoon liquid bleach in 1 quart of water. To make a bigger batch, mix 1/4 cup of bleach with 1 gallon of water. Remake the bleach solution every day. After 24 hours, it loses its power.

Although there may be state regulations regarding square footage per child for infants, the smaller space is sometimes preferable. Keep the scale of your infant room intimate. Everything should be kept within easy reach and distance. You should be able to see everywhere at once. The less clutter, the easier it is to negotiate the space and attend to the child's needs.

As the director of my center, I always make sure to assign a specific caregiver to a specific child. It's kind of like the buddy system. That's not to say that the caregiver doesn't attend to other children, or that the child doesn't get nurtured by other providers. It just offers the opportunity for some special bonding. I like to go with a natural fit. A lot of it is instinctive on my part. I get a feeling about an infant and a caregiver, and usually I'm really good about putting them together. If I'm not so good and I make a mistake, it's no biggie. I just mix it up until there is a fit that feels good. And you know what? In the end, there always is a "right" one. That's the nice thing about a center. Unlike the nanny-child situation where a bad fit could go on day after day, we at the center have enough diversity to experiment with combinations until we find the right one.

I've found that one of the most important principles when it comes to dealing with infants is to maximize their outdoor time. Fresh air and light is crucial to everyone, caregivers and babies alike. If they fall asleep when they're out in the stroller, that's fine too. Those outdoor naps are great for kids.

Don't feel that all the babies have to go outside at the same time. You can stagger the outdoor time all through the day, particularly if you're lucky to have some outdoor space right off the room like a backyard. If you do, then a few of the babies can go outside with a caregiver while others stay indoors.

Encourage parents to dress their children in outfits that are easy to change. What's easy for you is easy for everyone, and easy means less stress all around and more smiling! Snaps, for instance, are one of life's great inventions. So is Velcro. Tells parents to save all those wonderful outfits with lots of little buttons for special occasions.

The economics of child care is a major headache, but any way you can maximize the number of staff in the infant room is worth the effort. Infants needs as close to one-on-one care as possible.

When it comes to infants and food, start thinking really early in terms of "mealtime" rather than "feeding time." Eating, even for infants, is about a lot more than simple nutrition. It's a social experience, no matter what age you are. Or at least it should be!

Almost all babies have a certain time of day when they are difficult and fretful. Some people call it the "witching hour." For a lot of babies, it's the dinner hour when parents are frazzled and the baby's fretfulness just adds to the brew. But the difficult time can also happen at the child care center. Keep an eye out for patterns that emerge around a baby's difficult time of day. By anticipating it, you might be able to avert it, or, at least, you might be better equipped to handle it, knowing when it's coming.

Never forget that different babies have different temperaments. Some like a lot of action. Others like quiet. Some like to be held all the time. Others squirm until you put them down. The more you try to accommodate the different temperaments of the babies around you, the easier your life will be.

Don't forget that all caregivers have different temperaments also! Some caregivers are a great fit with some babies and not so great with others. Caregivers who like lots of action should team up with babies who like action. And if you end up caring for an infant who has a very different temperament from your own, try not to personalize it.

When I work with infants, I try to remind myself that treating them all the same is not treating them equally. Equal care means meeting everyone's needs, as individualistic as they might be.

Interaction with Toddlers

When children move from the infancy stage to toddlerhood, life is a whole new ball game. You want to be ready for anything, and armed with energy and understanding, as much of each as you can spare! Throughout this book, we've gathered lots of toddler-related tips, but what follows is more philosophical in nature; general remarks about toddlers from people who care for them.

Allow toddlers to say "no." That's a sign they're developing their identity and becoming their own persons. Don't take their "no's" personally, but don't feel you have to take orders from them either!

We all know about the "terrible twos." But, just as it is with teenagers, the press on the terrible twos is blown way out of proportion. It helps to think of it as the "terrific twos," when children are trying to become more independent and self-sufficient. There is a fair amount of challenging but as a caregiver, you can share in the excitement of their development, too. If the challenges are too constant, then you'll want to choose your battles. Is it worth a hassle just because little Jimmy has it in mind to wear his underwear on his head?

Automatically assume that everything will wind up in a toddler's mouth. Have a sink in the room so you can wash things easily.

Toddlers, as well as infants, should be able to bring something special from home for nap time or to show. It's not a thing to play with; it's more of a lovey or transitional object. It should be kept in the cubbie so it doesn't become something that the other children compete over.

Even if you stress flexibility, which I really try to, you still need to have consistency around certain things. Guns, for instance. I know some centers where toy guns are not a problem, but I don't like them and I don't allow them here. The kids know about it, and if they decide to turn a carrot into a gun, I'm not going to make a big fuss about it. But I do try to divert them from doing that kind of thing. Food is another issue that you need a clear message about. I don't let toddlers bring candy bars from home, for instance. Junk food just doesn't have a place in our center and everyone knows it.

Safety comes first. It's our number one concern. A parent's expectation and a child's expectation is that the center is a safe haven. If it's not, you shouldn't be in business. And a caregiver has to be on her toes and anticipate where danger may be coming from. Take peanut butter, for instance. You have to know that some children can be deathly allergic to peanuts. There's no room for slipups when it comes to a child's health and safety.

Keep allergy charts posted in the classroom and in the kitchen. The charts should include each child's name and picture so that all adults are aware of who is allergic to what. This can be a critical life or death issue and nothing should be left fuzzy.

Toddlers can be mean to each other. In our center, we follow Vivian Paley's rule: "You Can't Say

You Can't Play." It's just not allowed. The kids aren't always happy about it, but they accept it.

We talk about rules at circle time. We explain why we have them. For example, "If you walk around while you're eating, you could choke. That's why you have to sit down when you're eating." Kids like to talk about the rules at our center.

Keep your eyes open to competitive feelings among older toddlers. They all develop at such different rates. The key is to help them see that everyone is good at something. If the toddlers are old enough for circle time, a great topic of conversation could be What are you good at? What do you need help with?

We put a lot of emphasis on using our words, not pushing, fighting, or biting. That can be frustrating for kids who don't have as much language, but they get the idea. They can always just yell, "NO!"

Toddlers can be very intense about their activities. We try not to have scheduled times, but instead to let kids go from one activity to the next whenever they're ready. Children who are in the mood for dress-up can do it whenever they want. Kids who like to build might spend lots of time with blocks. And kids who love balls might be out in the park kicking a ball around. There's plenty of time later for bells ringing to signal the change of activities when they get to school!

Toddlers are passionate about their friends. We have lots of room for "special" friendships at our center, but that doesn't have to mean anyone gets left out. It's great for kids to love each other, and they can start learning at a really early age that loving your special friend doesn't mean you can't enjoy doing things with other children.

Some toddlers love naps. Others hate the whole idea of naps. We simply ask kids to have a quiet time. They lie on their cots, look at a book, or just rest and listen to soft music. We ask them to do that for at least a half-hour, and to respect the fact that some kids fall asleep and they have to be quiet until they wake up.

Toddlers and preschoolers can be very rigid about boy/girl stuff. Some boys just don't like to play with girls, and some girls only want to play with other girls. We always try to walk a fine line between respecting personal preferences and respecting each other. Everyone has to be treated with respect at our center.

One place we show respect for each other is around food. We never make fun of what someone else is eating, and we never force anyone to eat something they don't want to eat. We always have plenty of the basics around such as yogurt, veggies, and pasta. That way, we can make things everyone likes.

Toddlers and preschoolers can be fussy about privacy. Some of them have no problem dropping their pants to urinate on a tree. Others would sooner wet themselves than do that. Teachers need to know who they're dealing with and respect that.

We once had a child who was traumatized because he used to be in a child care center where they forced him to close his eyes at nap time. I don't even know if that's legal. It shouldn't be. Being forced to close your eyes can be very scary to little kids.

Interaction with Parents and Extended Family

Turn to our section on Getting Along in Chapter 8 for a whole lot of tips about teacher-parent teamwork. But for now, keep in mind that the center should be a place were all parents and family feel comfortable at any time of the day. Encourage them to visit. Encourage them to stay a while in the morning and come early at pick-up time. If parents and family are supportive, their kids will do better. If caregivers are supportive, parents will do better!

A group of parents at our center organized a baby-sitting co-op. They each put in a certain number of hours, and are entitled to the same number of hours in return. It works well for the kids because they're familiar with the parents, and it works well for the parents because they have a lot of confidence in each other. We've even had parents of toddlers use the baby-sitting co-op for sleepovers so they could have a child-free weekend.

Child care providers usually focus entirely on parents and children. But if you want to create a real sense of community, it helps to reach further than that. We have a family open house twice a year that includes siblings, grandparents, and any other people that are important in the life of the baby we're caring for. It's great for babies to see all the people they love in their child care center.

It's really easy to slip into thinking of family in the most traditional way, even though only one-quarter of all families in America today have a mom, a dad, and children. Try to be sensitive to different kinds of families right from the start. Some families might be single-mom or single-dad families. And there might be gay families with two moms or two dads. Babies and toddlers take everything in their stride. If you don't react to things like they're weird, the kids won't think they're weird.

During the year, we get snapshots of all the people who are important in our babies' lives and we hang them all over the walls. The kids look around and see that they're surrounded by each other's moms and dads and aunts and uncles and grandparents and siblings. We even have pictures of dogs and cats. They love it. It makes us feel like a great big family.

Lots of Stuff!

Child care centers are often the final resting places for everyone's odd mitten or boot. At the end of a year, you've got piles of clothing that need to find its way home. Every other month we have a lost and found day. We have a big table and we lay things out on it. Anything that doesn't get claimed is up for grabs. Next stop is Good Will.

We always encourage parents to donate things to our center when their children outgrow them. Then we put it all together to create a free store for people who need snowsuits and hats and other clothing. Everyone in the community is invited to come and shop in our free store. It makes us feel like a family.

There's lots of baby equipment that people only use for a very short time such as bassinets, infant seats, and infant swings. We keep a board in our center where people can list things they want to sell or trade. It's very useful and it offers another way for parents to connect with each other.

Stain Removal and Lots of Laundry

Very few stains are as difficult to remove as baby formula. People we spoke with suggest making a paste of meat tenderizer and cool water. Rub the paste into the stain and let it sit for a while. Then throw it in your washing machine the way you ordinarily would.

Bibs, bibs, bibs. If only we could wear them, too! Unless parents don't care at all about their baby's clothing, suggest that they get lots of soft, terry bibs. It makes life much easier, especially for droolers who end up with wet shirts and chafed chins.

 If parents notice any strange rashes on their young children, tell them to change their laundry detergent and see if the rashes go away. Babies have very sensitive skin and some laundry detergents are very harsh.

Chapter 13

BATTLING BURNOUT

hild care is great work—important, interesting, and emotionally rewarding— but it also can be very hard work. There is a lot of physical wear and tear. There are endless demands from needy little people. And then there is the low pay. All of this can lead to the dreaded "B" word: *Burnout.*

Many people abandon the child care field after they experience their first bout with burnout, and this is a great shame. For one thing, babies need stability. They need to develop relationships with their caregivers and they need to know that the same good, loving person will be there for them tomorrow who was there for them today.

Make no mistake about it: good people are hard to find. Good people who are talented with young children should be working with young children, not selling real estate or driving buses. While lobbying to increase wages and the esteem with which early childhood educators are regarded in our culture, we need to figure out ways to hang in there. The best way to do that is by turning to each other for help. By following the advice below, which we've gathered from child care providers like yourself, you can find ways to avoid burnout and reap the rewards of this magical field for many, many years.

Get A Life

As a caregiver, you've seen how hard transitions can be for children. Well, guess what? Many caregivers report difficulties making the transition back into their private lives at the end of their workday. Here are some ideas on how to make that transition easier.

Sometimes it can be really hard to go home to my own family in the evenings. After a whole day of dealing with other people's kids and all the demands being made on me, there I am, five minutes through my front door, and my husband and kids are making demands on me, too. For a while, I didn't think I could handle it. I thought about changing jobs. But then I learned a very important lesson: you have to stop work when the day is done. You've got to leave your job at the center and not come back to it until the following morning. Maybe after your own children go to sleep, you'll want to prep some materials or whatever for the next day, but nothing more intense than that. In other words, don't bring problems home with you. When you go home, get the goodies that *you* need and enjoy them!

I'm lucky enough to have a partner in my life, and if you can say the same, then make a point of talking to your partner at the end of the day. Too much of the time, people lead parallel lives, with not much getting said and little intimacy achieved. Talk to your partner. Encourage him or her to talk to you.

I always make it a point to sit down and talk to my kids at night. I ask them to tell me about the best part of their day and the worst part of their day. And then I tell them about mine. You'll see how much more effective this is at drawing people out than the open-ended "How was your day?" question. And whenever I have a good conversation with my own kids, I feel great.

One thing I have always done, even when my kids were little, was to let it be known that I needed a "time out" when I got home from work so that I could unwind. Now maybe some people think that's selfish, but, in fact, it's really a way of making myself more available, because without it, I'm no use at all. My rule was always that when I got home, I needed 20 minutes to myself before I started supper or did anything else. I used to show my children the big hand and the little hand on the clock, and I'd explain what 20 minutes looked like. They picked it up really quickly. The deal was that unless there was an emergency of some sort, those 20 minutes were sacred. For me, 20 minutes of just lying in bed and listening to the news on public radio was just what the doctor ordered. For everyone it's different, of course. One of my friends takes a shower. Another does 20 minutes of tai chi. Whatever works, I say!

I use my commute to decompress. I sit in the car, play loud music, and focus on nothing other than the road and the music. By the time I get home, I'm free from the day's hassles and ready to be with my family.

I managed to keep my sanity when I had young children at home, and I was taking care of young children at work, by establishing a regular bedtime for my kids. Come 8:30, they were in bed. It was good for them and great for me. At least that way, I knew I'd have some peaceful adult time for myself after some quality time with the kids.

When I get home from work, I put my phone machine on, and unless there's an absolute emergency, I don't take calls. My kids and my husband know that I'm there for them, and I know that they're there for me. We are our number one priority. The rest of the world just waits.

On my way home from work, I listen to books-on-tape in my car. It's a great transition for me into the adult world.

I live three miles from the child care center where I work, and most of the year, I jog home. Some of my coworkers think I'm nuts. They can't figure out how I can run after a long day of caring for kids, but for me it's the best. I run, I clear my mind, I come home, and head straight for the shower. By the time my husband gets home, I'm into my grown-up mode.

Taking Care of Yourself

Stress is an inevitable part of life when you work with children. There are a lot of demands on you and there are a lot of germs floating around that can sap your strength. We encourage caregivers to take a holistic approach to their lives and to make sure that they are getting everything they need.

First of all, you have to be able to recognize stress. Sometimes, it creeps up on you when you're not even paying attention, and then wham! you've got a whole lot of symptoms and you know that stress has you in its clutches. For me, the symptoms usually include neck pain, insomnia, and lack of appetite. Sometimes, I'll get really irritable or have mood swings. And when I'm stressed out, I have absolutely no interest in sex. But now I can recognize my "telltale signs" and periodically I'll take my temperature, so to speak, to see what symptoms are there, and to figure out just how much stress I'm carrying around and what I'm going to do about it.

It's so important to eat well. I avoid junk foods, anything highly processed, caffeine, and sugar. I try to eat a good variety of foods with lots of vegetables, fruits, and grains. The food we serve at the center is all good, nutritious, and well-balanced, so that helps a lot.

I make a point of hydrating. Water is the best thing for you. It's calorie-free, thirst-quenching, cheap, and good for you!

Don't forget regular exercise. I know how limited time can be, but you have to make room for it. My favorite is aerobic dance. Three or four times a week, I put on my favorite dance music—at the moment it's Santana—and for twenty minutes straight, I run, skip, hop, jump, slide, stretch, and bend. I can't imagine life without it!

If you're like me, exercise doesn't come naturally. In fact, most of the time, I hate it. But I've stuck with it now for a few years and it shows. You know what my secret is? The buddy system. I have a girlfriend who's my exercise "buddy." We meet three days a week after work and go for a brisk, three-mile walk in the neighborhood. If I try to poop out, she's on me, and I do the same for her.

Try to stay away from exercising late in the evening. Whenever I do, I'm up for hours.

Sleep, sleep, sleep. Do you realize how sleep-deprived we are as a nation? Human beings should get between eight and ten hours of sleep. Most of us are lucky if we get six. And it's almost impossible to make up that kind of deficit on the weekend. So go to bed early. For me, that means between nine and ten o'clock. My friends know not to call me late, and those who do get my machine.

Sometimes I'll have sleep problems. When I do, I'll just get up and read a book. I don't worry about it. It's the worrying about it that drives you crazy and keeps you up.

Everyone should have a hobby. It's the best kind of personal time there is. For me, it's my house plants. If I spend half an hour with them, I feel renewed. For other people, it's cooking, or maybe shopping for something they collect on Ebay, or teaching their dog ultimate Frisbee. That kind of concentrated time with something you enjoy is really invaluable.

I believe 100 percent in vacations. In other cultures, like in Europe, people get two or three times as much vacation as Americans get. Whatever vacation comes my way, I take. And, even if I don't go anywhere, I make a real vacation out of my vacation days. I force myself not to do any housework or anything else I don't like to do. Instead, I'll say to myself, Okay, You're having an Art week and I'll go to four different art museums that week. Or, if it's the middle of the winter, let's say, I'll tell myself, Welcome to Movie Week. And every day of my vacation I'll go see a film!

I use a behavior modification approach called reframing to alleviate my stress. That means I take an event, and I put another spin on it to make it into something better than what it first appears to be. A couple of years ago, for example, I was fired from the center where I worked. I never got along well with the director who was a mega control freak. It was a bad time for me to be fired because I had a lot of expenses, but I reframed it. I told myself that this was the beginning of good new things, and an avenue out of bad, old things. And guess what? It was!

My best antistress solution is yoga. If you haven't discovered it yet, you owe it to yourself to get with it. Take a class, or if you can't do that, rent a yoga video. You'll be amazed at how it gets your stress under control and makes your body feel better than it has in years.

For me, a lot of my stress used to come out of feeling that I was being taken advantage of. That's my problem, I know—I was the classic middle child—but I've found a way around it. Now when I'm in a situation, I use three key phrases to try to find out where I am with something. I feel, I want, I will. For instance, I'll say, *I feel* that it would be a mistake for me to take on more responsibility now, so I'm not going to take on the associate director job. However, I *want* to keep the possibility open for the future. I *will* talk to the director about it and let her know that when I feel ready, I will consider it, if she will still consider me.

Once or twice a year I buy myself a massage. For me, it's the ultimate luxury. In fact, when anyone asks what I want for a special gift, I always suggest they chip in with other friends and get me a massage.

I always do something totally adult-oriented at least twice a week. During the week, I enroll in a course. It's great if it's a course that has nothing to do with kids like art history or film. I go and sit with other adults and really enjoy their company. On the weekends, I always go to a museum, go out to dinner with friends, or go hiking, something that I really enjoy with people I enjoy.

 Organize Yourself

Some people burn out from all the stress that comes from being poorly organized. The feeling of being habitually behind the eight ball is not a pleasant one, and the amount of denial and avoidance that's involved can be exhausting.

Don't procrastinate (although almost everyone does)! The best thing is to set a deadline for yourself: "On May 14, I will start studying for my certification." A concrete date is a lot better than words like "soon," "before long," "before you know it," or any of the other empty things we tell ourselves.

I find the best defense against procrastination is to start out with something easy. For instance, I have an absolutely horrible time getting my taxes done every year. It's just something I'm really, really bad at. Once I was four months late, I had to pay penalties, and I was scared to death that the IRS was going to come after me. Since then, I've used the following technique. Each day, for about a month before April 15, I give myself assignments of increasing difficulty. I'll start with something easy, like sharpening pencils, and then I'll go on to the next level of difficulty, which might be to go through a box of receipts. And by the time midnight rolls around on April 15, I'm done!

My secret weapon against procrastination is a reward. If I have to do something I really don't like to do, like clean the oven, for instance, I'll "give" myself a treat afterwards, like an ice cream cone. It's the carrot in front of the donkey bit, and it's incredibly effective.

Prioritize, prioritize, prioritize. If you're taking on an extra job—let's say hosting a wedding shower for a coworker—there's more chance of it being completed if you prioritize. That means you might create a chart of A jobs, B jobs, and C jobs, getting the A jobs done first. The A jobs might be sending out the invitations and ordering the champagne. The B jobs might be vacuuming your apartment if that's where the party is going to be held, and ironing the outfit you're going to wear. The C jobs are all the little Martha Stewart extras like wrapping rosebuds around the candles or whatever. If there's time, fine. If not, so you won't call me Martha. Big deal.

I live by lists. Without them, I would be a puddle. Every day I jot down a "to do" list. Get the dog's medicine. Cancel the rented car. Call Aunt Sally for her birthday. Examine my breasts. Whatever. And I don't go to sleep at night (well, most nights) until each item is checked off.

Learn the most important word in the English language: NO. You also can learn to say it in a way that doesn't put people off. It's critical not to allow yourself to become overburdened by other people's demands and expectations.

I never spend time anymore with people I'm not interested in being with. My time is too valuable. I just can't waste it. That may sound snobby, but it isn't. I have very dear friends that I almost never get to see, and I spend a lot of my time at work. I simply have to treat my time like the precious commodity that it is.

I've used a planner for years. A lot of people I know are switching over to those electronic planners, but I do just fine with my pocket calendar. The important thing, however, when you use a planner, is to factor into your day what's called "response time." That means some free time so that when the unexpected happens, you can shift your schedule and accommodate it. For instance, if your mother's car breaks down and you have to pick her up at the garage, you can use that "response time" to get the task done or else shift something else into that response time slot.

One of the most important lessons I've learned to help me avoid burnout is to make use of unexpected gifts of time. They do happen (snow days, for instance), and when they do, you have to treat them as the wonderful little miracles they are. Maybe it's the time when you can get something done you've been putting off like cleaning up the laundry room. Or maybe you'll play a board game with your kids who often feel that there's never enough time to play games with you. Whatever you do, taste the sweetness of it.

As far as I'm concerned, the best antidote to burnout is what's called simplicity. There are a lot of books out on the subject now. It means a way of looking at life where "less is more." Use shortcuts. Don't run yourself ragged. Smell the flowers. Weed out the inconsequential, the excessive, and the useless, and discover what's really meaningful to you.

I think everyone should be entitled to two "mental health" days. In other words, two days a year. You don't need to be "sick" to call in sick. Then, use the days for anything your heart desires. Stay in your PJs all day long. Get dressed up and visit a friend you haven't seen in ages. Plan it ahead of time or do it spontaneously. Just play hooky!

What the Child Care Center Can Do to Battle Burnout

As with any workplace, the child care center has to take into account the psychological, ergonomic, and health issues of its workers. Some important points to take into account include the following.

Time on the floor is very important in developing the muscles of young children, but it can be taxing on the muscles of adults. Make it comfortable for adults to be on the floor. Have lots of pillows that adults can lean back on. Just make sure to remove them when adults aren't there so they don't present a danger.

Nurture the friendships among your staff. Offer staff development and encourage friends to take courses together.

If you have a staff member with a particular talent—singing, painting, acting—find ways to incorporate it into your program.

Never miss an opportunity to give a fellow caregiver positive feedback.

A caregiver's back is susceptible to strain, given all the lifting and carrying she has to do. Everything must be done to help protect the caregiver's back. Changing tables and cribs should always be kept at the right height. Stools should be on hand for shorter workers to stand on. An ounce of prevention is worth a pound of cure.

Infant caregivers need regular breaks but they have to understand that they need to be flexible about taking those breaks. If you're putting an infant to sleep, you don't look at your watch and say "Break!" in the middle of what you're doing.

Caregivers need to support each other. It's fine for them to talk to each other as they go about their work. With three- and four-year olds, it isn't fine. There the dialogue should be between caregiver and child. But with infants, it is appropriate to have colleague talk, which protects against the isolation that comes from working with infants.

Caregivers can include the infants in their talk. For instance, they might say, "Yes, that's Karen talking to me about what she's going to have for dinner tonight." This clues infants into the rhythms and patterns of conversation.

Make sure that the music you play isn't all kids' music. Adults can go a little nutty if they're listening to "Three Blind Mice" or "Frere Jacques" all day long. Mix it up. Have some traditional children's music along with some Bach, some Dolly Parton, and some Ella Fitzgerald. This way, you create an environment that is pleasant for caregiver and child alike.

Invest in good lighting. Have a fund-raiser if you need it because quality lighting makes a difference. Light that is too dim, gives off a ghostly glow, or that is harsh and cold can make a great difference in the moods of everyone at the center.

If there's ever a problem between a parent and a caregiver, always make certain to talk to your staff privately about it. They need your support, even if they've made a mistake. Then, find a way to help them make peace with the parent.

Make sure you have comfortable places to sit such as a good sofa, some rockers, or some sturdy chairs. It's a long day, and people need their creature comforts.

Everything about infant care is about routine. You're constantly changing diapers, feeding, and putting infants down for their nap, so the trick is to make the routines rich and to mix them up with nice surprises. Find some funny songs to play on the CD player. Buy some pizzas at the end of the week. Splurge on fresh flowers every now and then. Make a movie. Have a St. Patrick's Day party to get you through March. Have a Thursday party to get you through the rest of the week. Do whatever works to stave off the humdrum and to keep everyone fresh and engaged.

Make staff training an ongoing part of your program. That means time for infant caregivers to talk about what infant caregiving is like. That means real developmental education that makes a caregiver's work much more interesting and validates what she's doing. And then there's supervision and constructive feedback so that a caregiver's performance can reach its full potential.

Always talk about your staff with respect when you're talking to kids and to their parents. The work they do is genuinely noble.

INDEX

exercise helps, 239
put on the phone machine, 239
take "time out" to unwind, 237–238
talk to your family at night, 237
use your commute to decompress, 238